POP-UP
design and paper mechanics

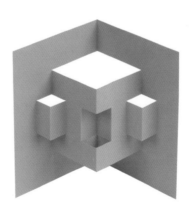

**HOW TO MAKE
FOLDING PAPER
SCULPTURE**

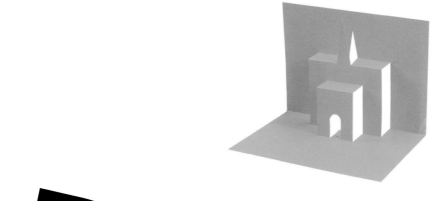

POP-UP
design and paper mechanics

**HOW TO MAKE
FOLDING PAPER
SCULPTURE**

Duncan Birmingham

GUILD OF MASTER
CRAFTSMAN PUBLICATIONS

For Anne – who decorated
some of the pop-ups.

First published 2010 by
Guild of Master Craftsman Publications Ltd
Castle Place, 166 High Street, Lewes,
East Sussex BN7 1XU

Reprinted 2011

Text © Duncan Birmingham, 2010
Copyright in the Work © GMC Publications Ltd, 2010

ISBN: 978-1-86108-685-3

A catalogue record for this book is available from
the British Library.

Publisher Jonathan Bailey
Production Manager Jim Bulley
Managing Editor Gerrie Purcell
Project Editor Gill Parris
Managing Art Editor Gilda Pacitti
Designer Luke Herriott
Photographer Anthony Bailey

Set in ITC Avant Garde Gothic (T1) and Clarendon
Colour origination by GMC Reprographics
Printed and bound in China by C & C Offset

contents

Introduction.........................8

getting started

How to use this book 12

Terms used 13

Materials.............................14

Working practice............................16

The simple rules of pop-up 18

The underlying pop-up structures...20

Pop-up sketching............................24

High-quality pop-ups 26

foundation shapes

1   Right-angle V-fold 30

2   Acute-angle V-fold..................... 32

3   Pointed V-fold 34

4   Obtuse-angle V-fold 36

5   Asymmetric V-fold..................... 38

6   Parallel-folds............................ 42

7   Parallelogram 46

8   Asymmetric parallel-folds.......... 50

9   Zigzag-fold................................ 52

10 M-fold.. 56

11 Floating plane 60

12 Box 64

13 Open-topped shapes 68

14 Pyramids.................................... 72

15 Curved shapes 76

16 Twisting mechanism 80

17 Automatic pull-strip 82

18 Moving arms............................. 88

building techniques

1 Cutting parts away 96

2 Sticking pieces on 98

3 Extra creases 102

4 Angle-folded strips 106

5 Counter-folds 108

6 Slots 116

7 Bending planes 122

8 Straps 124

9 45-degree folds 126

pull-tab mechanisms

1 Pull-strips 132

2 Pivots 134

3 Flaps 136

project templates

1 House 146

2 Garden 148

3 Lunch 150

4 Horse 152

5 Dancers 154

6 Aeroplane 156

7 Reclining figure 158

8 Bird 160

9 Boat 162

10 Flower 164

11 Fish 166

12 Runner 168

13 Car 170

14 Dragon 172

About the author 174

Index 175

Introduction

This book introduces an entirely fresh approach to the intriguing field of pop-up. It provides a simple method for building complicated pop-up structures and it distils the apparently daunting menagerie of pop-up mechanisms into a logical set of basic shapes.

Paper mechanics is approached as a sculptural skill that needs only card, scissors, glue and a minimal theoretical understanding. With this method you can make spectacular, complex, experimental pop-ups without the need for laborious measuring, scoring and technical drawing.

All the key mechanisms found in commercial pop-up books and cards are explained: these are the Foundation Shapes, the structures at the core of pop-up spreads. Each mechanism is examined individually with explanations of how to make it and its derivative variations. The underlying geometric theory necessary for transforming pop-up sketches into sophisticated, high-quality designs is also explained.

The second half of the book is devoted to ways of working with the Foundation Shapes: how to build on the foundations and how to modify and extend them. There is also a chapter on mechanisms activated by pulling a tab, which slide, turn and flip. These can be used on their own but more often are incorporated into a three-dimensional spread to give it some extra action.

At the end of the book there is a series of Projects. These are templates for pop-up models demonstrating how the Foundation Shapes can be used, combined and developed.

Although this book aims to simplify and demystify the field of pop-up, it is still a complex art. It is best to start at the beginning of the book and work through it, so that practical skills develop along with theoretical understanding. A complete set of the Foundation Shapes and Projects can be assembled – by gluing their bases back to back – to produce a three-dimensional pop-up dictionary.

getting started

This book introduces a method for making exciting and surprising pop-ups quickly and easily with only card, scissors, glue and some very simple techniques. However, before you start building, there is some basic information that all pop-up designers need to know.

This chapter covers that fundamental knowledge:

→ Understanding the practicalities – a few technical words, the basic materials, some tricks of the trade – makes both construction and following the instructions easier.

→ The underlying principles of paper mechanics are very simple – understanding these can help to avoid difficulties when designs start getting complex.

→ For highly complex designs, having an overview of the three-dimensional possibilities can both resolve difficulties and inspire new ideas.

How to use this book

This book offers a logical analysis of the complex field of pop-up structures. It is also a guide showing simple ways to build the mechanisms involved. If new to the subject, it is advisable to work through the book from the beginning, so learning both practical skills and theoretical understanding simultaneously.

Getting started
(pages 10–27)

Read this section first to get an overview of the subject: the tools, the shapes, the techniques, the practicalities and the possibilities.

Foundation shapes
(pages 28-93)

This chapter introduces the mechanisms that raise almost all the pop-up designs found in books and cards. When making these it is best to start at the beginning to get a sound understanding of the principles involved. As you build these pop-ups, you can stick their bases back-to-back to build up a pop-up reference book. Making them into a booklet keeps them in order, makes them easier to access and prevents them from getting damaged.

Diagrams
(throughout)

Throughout the book construction methods are explained in a series of numbered steps. Diagrams are numbered with their corresponding steps. Not all steps have diagrams.

Building techniques
(pages 94–129)

This explains the range of possible transformation techniques. After making each Foundation Shape look at this section for ways of extending, modifying and building on the shape.

Pull-tab mechanisms
(pages 130–139)

These two-dimensional mechanisms are part of every paper engineer's repertoire. Use them to produce surprising action on a flat page, or add them to pop-up spreads to introduce an interactive element to three-dimensional designs.

Project templates
(pages 140–173)

These are the templates for a set of models, which demonstrate how to combine the mechanisms to create complex pop-up designs. They can be made up as one-off pop-up cards, or they too can be glued together to form a second, 'advanced' reference booklet.

Terms used

This book aims to be easy for anyone to read and understand without the need for any specialist knowledge. However, since pop-up involves three-dimensional geometry, a few technical and mathematical terms do have to be used. If you come across any unfamiliar terms this brief guide should help to make things clear.

Acute angle Angle less than 90°

Base Double page on which pop-ups are built

Dummy Rough, working model, for testing design ideas

Gluing-tab The small flap on which glue is spread

Gully A fold line that closes (or flattens out) as the base is closed

Mountain-fold ('M') A crease that comes forward towards the viewer

Mechanism Pop-up structure

Net Flat plan of a pop-up piece

Obtuse angle Angle greater than 90°

Parallelogram Four-sided figure: opposite sides are parallel and equal

Plane Flat surface of a piece of card

Quadrilateral Four-sided figure

Right angle 90° angle

Score line A dent in the card that helps it fold sharply and accurately

Slits and slots A slit is a simple cut in the card: a slot is $1/16$–$1/8$ in (1.5–3mm) wide

Spine-fold Central crease down the middle of the base card

Spread Double page with a pop-up built onto it

Sticking strip Area that a gluing-tab is stuck to

Valley-fold ('V') A crease that goes back, away from the viewer

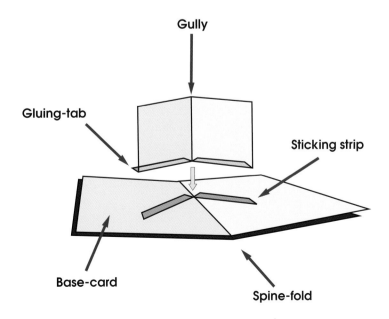

Gully · Gluing-tab · Sticking strip · Base-card · Spine-fold

Materials

To make most of the pop-ups in this book you need only card, scissors and glue.
The more complex mechanisms need a scoring tool, a ruler and (for a very few) a
compass. Drawing instruments are rarely required, except for drawing up the nets
of precisely engineered designs, in which case a protractor and set square are vital.

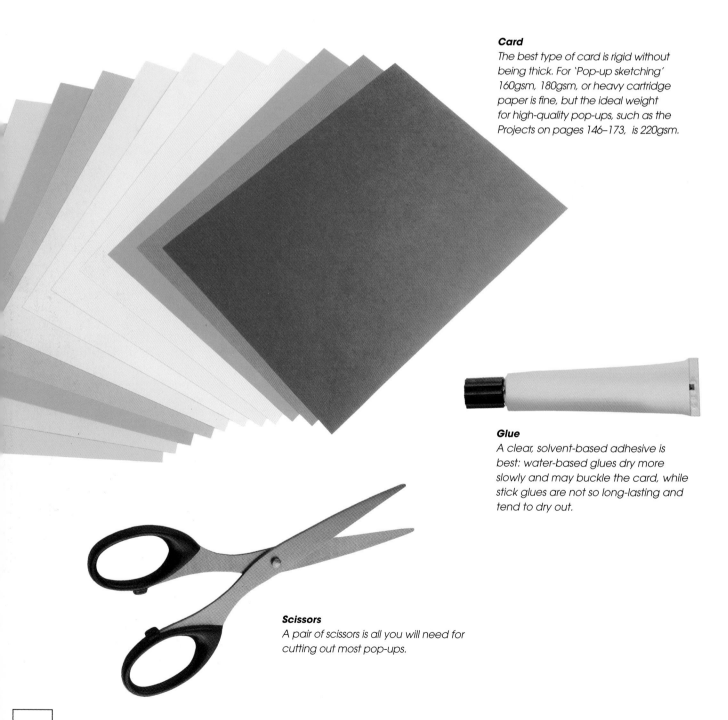

Card
*The best type of card is rigid without
being thick. For 'Pop-up sketching'
160gsm, 180gsm, or heavy cartridge
paper is fine, but the ideal weight
for high-quality pop-ups, such as the
Projects on pages 146–173, is 220gsm.*

Glue
*A clear, solvent-based adhesive is
best: water-based glues dry more
slowly and may buckle the card, while
stick glues are not so long-lasting and
tend to dry out.*

Scissors
*A pair of scissors is all you will need for
cutting out most pop-ups.*

Craft-knife

To make slots, sophisticated pop-ups and pull-tab mechanisms, a craft-knife, or scalpel, is essential. The type of knife, which has an extending snap-off blade, is excellent.

Pencil

Make sure pencils are sharp. A propelling, or 'clutch', pencil is ideal.

Scoring

A ball-point pen without ink is best for this – it is precise, easy to use and makes a stronger fold by compressing the card's fibres rather than cutting them. The rounded end of a paper clip could also be used.

Ruler

Use a ruler for scoring straight creases as well as for measuring. A metal ruler is best for making long, straight cuts.

Eraser

This can be used for removing excess (newly dry) glue as well as pencil marks.

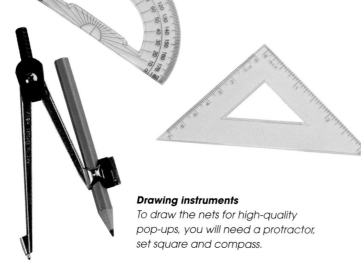

Drawing instruments

To draw the nets for high-quality pop-ups, you will need a protractor, set square and compass.

Cutting-mat

A commercial, self-healing mat like the one above is best. Failing that, thick cardboard (e.g. the back of a drawing pad) is adequate.

Working practice

Building pop-ups does require some technical finesse. Following these practical guidelines will enhance your pop-ups and help you avoid some common pitfalls.

Measuring

Most of the models in this book can be made quickly without measuring. High-quality pop-ups have to be accurately measured – when measuring lengths or angles, the measurement is always from crease to crease (not to the edge of the card).

Cutting

Scissors are fine for most of the cutting you will need to do. However, for 'windows', slots, fiddly work and pull-strips, a craft-knife is essential.

Folding and scoring

Always crease every fold very thoroughly: fold, crimp, fold the crease back on itself, then crimp again. An insufficiently creased fold will be inflexible and will inhibit the pop-up's movement and distort its shape.

The folds on most of the models in this book can be made 'freehand', without scoring, but a fold that has not been scored must be especially thoroughly creased. Lighter card (160–180gsm), such as photocopy card or heavy cartridge paper, is easiest to work with.

The crisp and precise creases on finely worked pop-up models are made by measuring and scoring the lines. Heavier card makes a more sturdy model, but it must be scored.

The exact position of the folds is the key to the success of three-dimensional paper mechanisms. The shape of the cut edges is usually mechanically unimportant and only relevant to the visual design.

Gluing-tabs

Gluing-tabs should be at least $^3/_8$ in (1cm) wide, as narrow tabs tend to pull off. Gluing-tabs can point forwards or backwards, be hidden, or show as part of the design. The position of the crease is the important aspect of the mechanism.

V-fold with tabs pointing backwards.

V-fold with tabs pointing forward.

Parallelogram with tabs pointing backwards.   *Parallelogram with tabs pointing forward.*

Gluing

Smear glue on the tabs – not on the surface the tabs will be glued to – right up to the edge of the crease: use a small piece of card or a finger for this – the little finger is good as it tends not to be used for picking other things up, so is less messy. After sticking each piece in place, shut the base and then press firmly. This will ensure that the structure is sound at every step of the construction.

Gluing method
The gluing method used throughout this book ensures that gluing-tabs are stuck down symmetrically on the base. This symmetry is very important.

Gluing V-folds

1 Put glue on one tab and stick it to the page. Ensure the pop-up's central crease is touching the central gully of the page.

2 Fold the pop-up piece into its closed position. Put glue on the other gluing-tab.

3 Close the page and press firmly, then open out to check the pop-up.

Gluing Parallel-folds

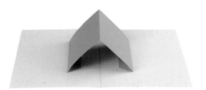

1 Put glue on one tab and stick it to the page, making sure the pop-up's creases are parallel to the central gully of the page.

2 Fold the pop-up piece into its closed position. Put glue on the other gluing-tab.

3 Close the page and press firmly, then open out to check the pop-up.

Base-cards
Every model in this book is built on a base.

Making a base-card

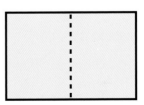

1 Take a sheet of A4 card.

2 Fold it in half and crease very thoroughly.

3 Open the card to form the base, with central crease.

The simple rules of pop-up

Underlying virtually all pop-up designs there are two principle mechanisms, V-folds and Parallel-folds. Even the most intricate and complex design will be made using permutations and combinations of these two. The three fundamental rules that always apply to both these types of mechanism are explained below.

1 Every pop-up must span a gully

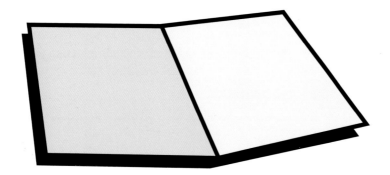

The first gully is the spine-fold down the middle of the base-card. It is this gully opening, as the page is opened, that powers (or raises) the pop-up.

2 Pop-ups must be balanced on each side of the gully

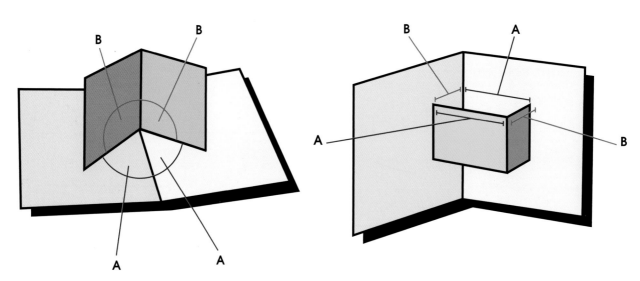

On V-folds the angles balance. Angles **A** + **B** on the left of the gully = angles **A** + **B** on the right of the gully.

On Parallel-folds the lengths balance. Lengths **A** + **B** on the left of the gully = lengths **A** + **B** on the right of the gully.

3 Every pop-up creates gullies and more pop-ups can be built into these gullies

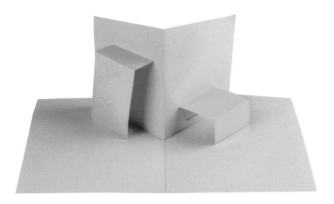

V-fold lifting Parallelograms that span the gullies created where the V-fold is attached to the base.

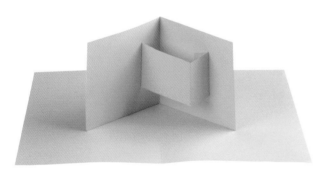

V-fold lifting a Parallelogram spanning the gully created by the central crease of the pop-up.

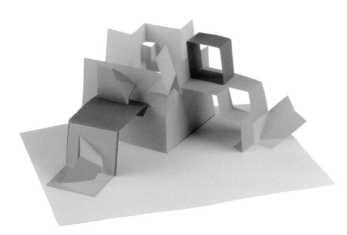

V-fold lifting an array of secondary pop-ups. These additional pop-ups also create gullies and more pop-ups can be built into them.

GULLIES

Where a pop-up plane is attached to the base, two gullies are created, **A** and **B**. As the base closes and the pop-up piece folds down, gully **A** flattens out open and gully **B** folds closed, so, in most cases, only type **B** gullies are suitable for building into. When adding to a pop-up spread, make sure that any gullies you are building into are type **B**.

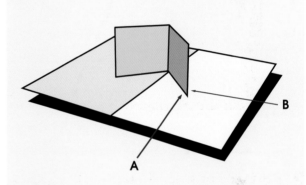

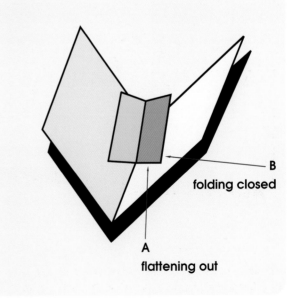

The underlying pop-up structures

These 18 structures are the building blocks of pop-up – the Foundation Shapes. Almost every pop-up design will have a version of one of these shapes at its core, spanning the spine-fold and providing the 'lift' that raises the pop-up structure.

The Primary Foundation Shapes

The Primary Foundation Shapes are the basic forms of the V-fold and the Parallel-fold. They all have just two planes and three creases: two where the piece is attached to the page, and one above the spine.

V-folds

On V-folds all the creases converge at the same point on the spine.

1 Right-angle V-fold

2 Acute-angle V-fold

3 Pointed V-fold

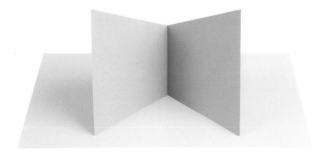

4 Obtuse-angle V-fold

5 Asymmetric V-fold

Parallel-folds

On Parallel-folds all the creases are parallel to the spine.

6 Parallel-fold

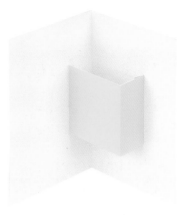

7 Parallelogram

8 Asymmetric Parallel-fold

The head is made with an Acute-angle V-fold, the nose is a Pointed V-fold, and the hat is made with an Angle-folded strip (pages 106–107) which is attached to the head using Building Technique 3.5 (page 105).

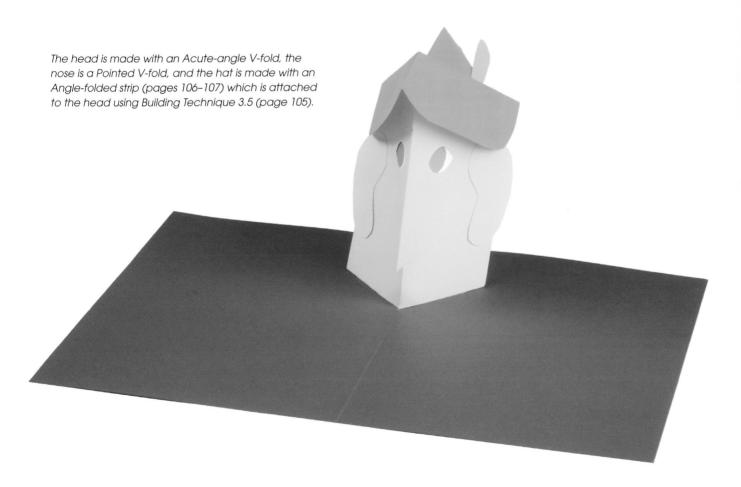

The Secondary Foundation Shapes

The Secondary Foundation Shapes are derived from the Primary Shapes. They have more creases and more gullies, so are slightly more complex. They are often deployed in this most basic form, but their deeper potential lies in the ways that they can be used to raise planes, or create gullies wherever the paper engineer desires.

Shapes 9 and 10 are based on V-folds

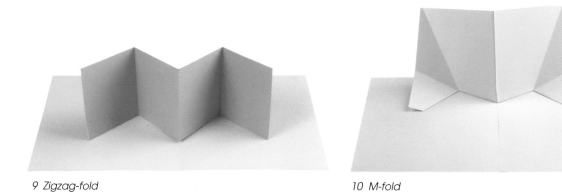

9 Zigzag-fold

10 M-fold

Shapes 11 and 12 are composed of multiple Parallel-folds

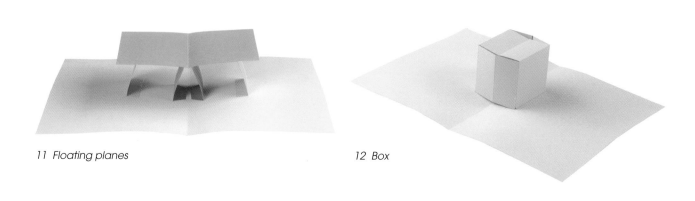

11 Floating planes

12 Box

All the shapes are very versatile and easy to modify: their dimensions can be altered; creases can be added; parts can be cut away; and extra pieces can be stuck on. They can also be combined with each other.

The key to successful pop-up design lies in understanding the Foundation Shapes: their individual characteristics; how each can be used to raise planes and gullies in different places and at different angles on the page; how they move; how they fold away; and the limitations of each mechanism.

Shapes 13, 14 and 15 can be based on either V-folds or Parallel-folds

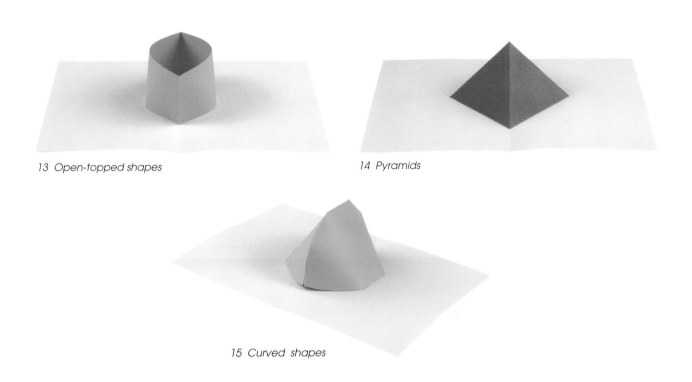

13 Open-topped shapes

14 Pyramids

15 Curved shapes

Shapes 16, 17 and 18 produce unusual or surprising actions

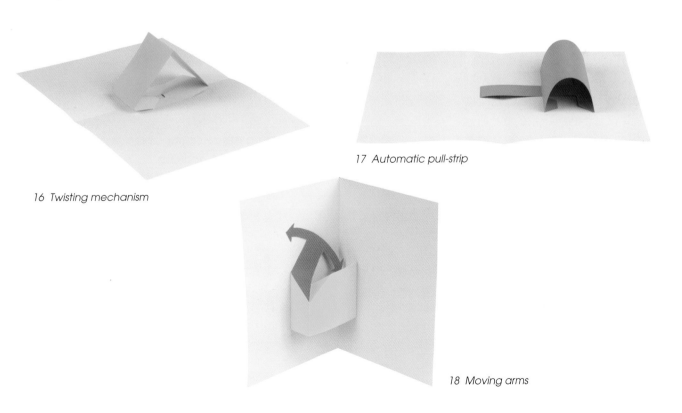

16 Twisting mechanism

17 Automatic pull-strip

18 Moving arms

Pop-up sketching

Pop-up sketching is a way of building three-dimensional pop-up models in a free and spontaneous way. There is no need to draw up a plan first. Lengths and angles don't need to be measured. The main consideration is to use card that is rigid enough to pop-up but thin enough not to need scoring: 160gsm is perfect, but 120–200gsm also works.

- **Start with a Foundation Shape**
  Either find a mechanism that lends itself to your subject, or choose an intriguing shape.

- **Make the Foundation Shape and then experiment with it**
  A three-dimensional model makes it easier to visualize how to develop a pop-up idea. It also makes any design problems clear.

- **Cut parts of the pop-up piece away**
  'Windows', slots and other holes in the pop-up are best cut out using a craft-knife before the piece is stuck to the base. Once a piece has been glued into position, trimming it with a pair of scissors can be very effective.

- **Stick extra pieces on**
  These can be simple, flat planes which jut out over the edge of the pop-up, or they can be small three-dimensional pieces (see pages 98–101 and 106–115). A small pop-up can be the muscle that lifts a big image.

- **Add extra creases**
  This technique can be used both to modify a Foundation Shape and as a way to generate more planes and gullies for building on. Extra creases have to be added before the piece is stuck to the base (see pages 102–105).

- **Build more pop-ups onto the gullies created by a Foundation Shape**
  These create yet more planes and gullies which can in turn be extended.

- **Make more than one version to test and refine ideas**
  All the shapes presented here are examples of configurations – they don't have specific lengths or angles. Experiment with sizes of lengths and angles – the same configuration can produce a broad range of results.

- **Stick pop-up models back-to-back to make reference booklets**
  When gluing these together, align the spines of the cards. Keeping models in this form protects them and makes them more accessible.

The Building Techniques chapter (pages 94–129) explores all these methods in greater depth.

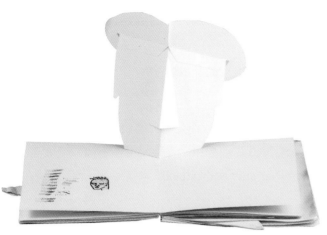

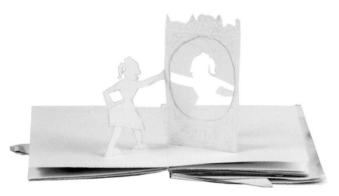

This face is made with an Acute-angle V-fold, the nose with a Pointed V-fold.

This is a simple Right-angle V-fold, with parts cut away.

PROBLEM SOLVING

If a newly glued-on piece doesn't work:
Pull it off before the glue sets. Adjust it, then stick it on again.

If part of a complex construction is unsatisfactory:
Cut it away and replace it.

If a tab has torn off:
Make a scored and folded 'hinge' to replace it.

When a pop-up piece has become creased in the wrong place:
Stick on a patch of card to strengthen the plane.

When a pop-up experiment grows so big that it no longer fits within the base:
Glue bigger pieces of card onto the outside of the base.

An adapted M-fold – the outer arms have been added to the outer planes so that they jut forward.

High-quality pop-ups

Pop-ups made with heavier card, those that are highly illustrated, or designs for reproduction, all need to be drawn up as a net indicating the precise lengths and angles. To do this a protractor, set square, compass and ruler are required.

Converting three-dimensional sketches into high-quality pop-ups

Your pop-up sketches may be as good as you want to achieve but, if you want to refine designs and produce high-quality pop-ups, you have to draw up nets for the pop-up pieces.

As a guide to making an exact shape use:

- your pop-up sketches
- the project templates at the end of this book
- spreads found in pop-up books.

Transfer angles and lengths from the models to your drawing of the net. Throughout the book, the boxes marked 'theory' explain the necessary geometry.

When drawing up a net, the fold lines on an experimental design made with several pieces of card can often be translated into an elegant, complex, one piece pop-up.

Here a V-fold is used to raise Parallelograms. This mechanism is explained in 7.2 (page 49) but in that case an Acute V-fold is used and in this example it is a Right-angle V-fold.

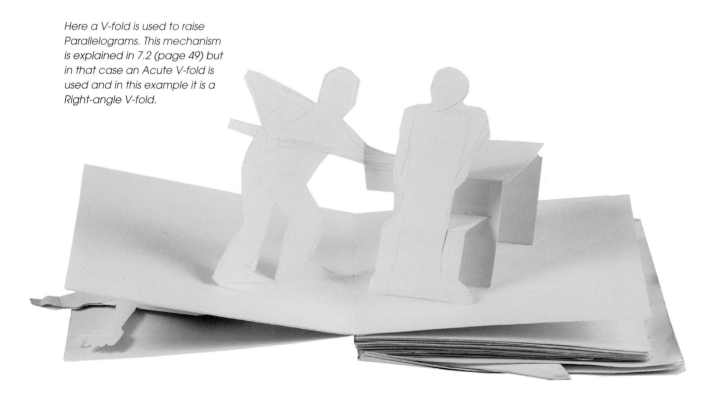

Using card to measure angles on a three-dimensional model

To measure an awkward angle on a pop-up model, use a piece of scrap card.

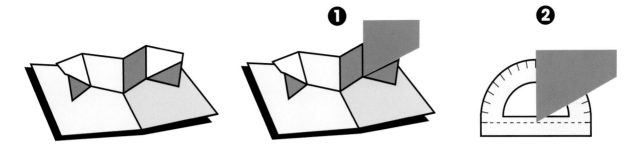

1 Trim the card until it fits into the angle to be measured.

2 Use a protractor to measure the angle on the piece of card.

3 Draw the angle onto the plan of the high quality pop-up – the card may be used as a template to draw the angle directly onto the net.

The same system can be used to measure awkward lengths on a model.

Working order for high-quality pop-ups

1 Draw the net.

2 Illustrate the pieces: either use conventional colouring materials, or decorate with anything that will go flat, such as tissue paper, wool, foil, photographs, fabric and feathers.

3 Score – this is easiest to do while the pieces are still part of a big piece of card.

4 Cut out.

5 Fold and crease thoroughly.

6 Glue pieces on one at a time. Close the base and press firmly after adding each piece to ensure that all folds and sticking points are sound.

PROBLEM SOLVING

Be precise. Problems with quality pop-ups usually stem from a lack of precision, careless measuring, or messy gluing.

Check that:
- You fully understand the geometric theory.
- The angles of score lines are exact.
- Parallel creases are parallel.
- Folds are thoroughly creased.
- Glue: this needs to be controlled so that it doesn't ooze; it also needs to be thoroughly spread, right up to the edge of a fold.
- The card is the right weight for the design.

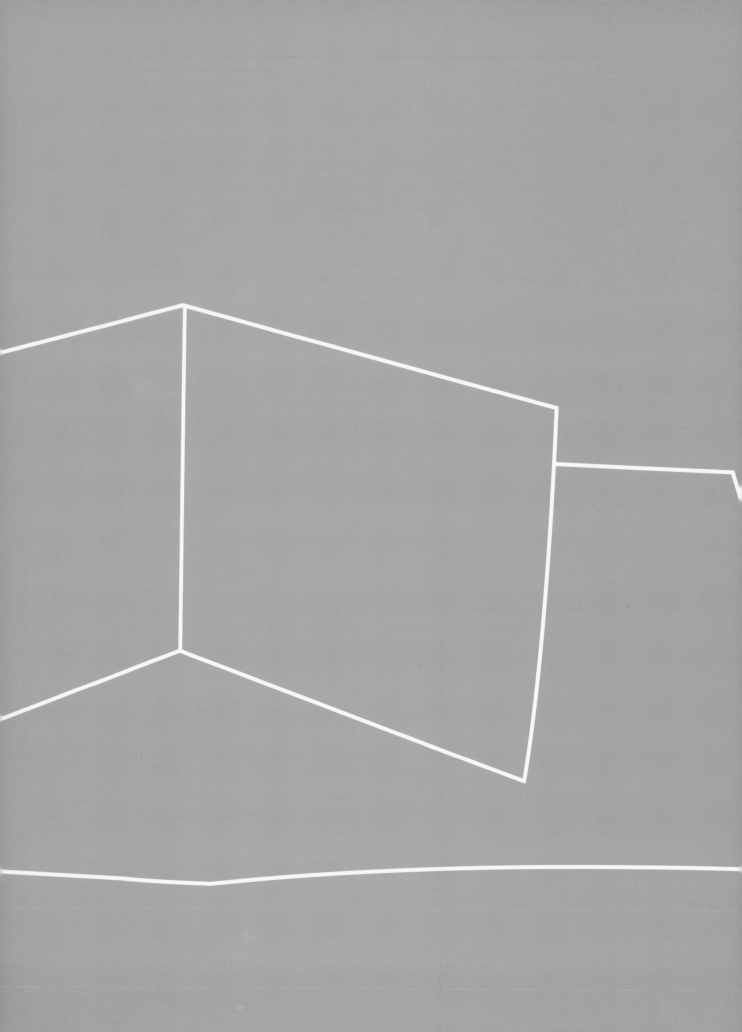

foundation shapes

The 18 mechanisms included here are the building blocks of pop-up. An effective design can be created using just one, standing alone, or several can be combined to create highly complex structures. Almost always, though, one of these will be at the core, spanning the spine and generating the movement as the spread is opened.

→ With Foundation Shapes, each mechanism is an abstract configuration of planes and gullies, has individual sculptural potential and can support and raise extensions in subtly different ways.

→ They should not be treated as fixed shapes, only to be approached from the angle at which they are photographed in this book. None of them has a fixed front, back, top or sides.

→ When designing, look at each shape from all angles. Consider using it with the base as a 'ground' from which the pop-up rises, or have the base as a background with the pop-up coming forward from it.

→ Try making several examples of any shape that intrigues you. By using different lengths, angles and proportions, the same configuration can be made taller, shorter, wider or steeper.

Other ways of modifying, extending and developing the Foundation Shapes are explored in the chapter on Building Techniques (pages 94–129).

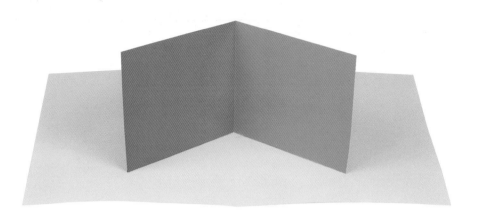

Foundation Shape 1

Right-angle V-fold

The Right-angle V-fold is the most straightforward to make. It is normally used pointing away from the viewer and near the front of the page.

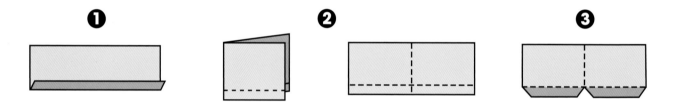

1 Make a fold about ½in (15mm) away from the bottom edge of a piece of card.

2 Fold vertically – this one does not have to be in the centre – then open out.

3 Trim the two gluing-tabs to shape, as shown above.

These two photos show narrow-angle and wide-angle gluing options for identical V-fold pieces.

All V-folds fold down in the direction in which they are pointing. Put tall Right-angle V-folds near the front, or bottom, of the spread

GLUING

Before gluing, experiment with the possible angles of the piece on the page: acute angles give a sharp, narrow pop-up; wider angles make a broader shape. Having decided upon the shape you'd like to create, glue the piece to the page (see 'Gluing' instructions on page 17).

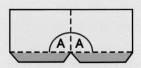

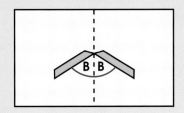

On the pop-up piece, angles **A** are both 90°.

On the page, angles **B** are the same as each other; they must be less than 90°.

Note the balance: the angles on the left **A** + **B** = the angles on the right **A** + **B**.

A POSSIBLE PROBLEM: THE 'SAGGING' V-FOLD

1 The Right-angle V-fold is best used pointing away from the viewer.

2 When it points towards the viewer it tends to 'sag' unless the base is absolutely flat. To correct the 'sag' modify the angles on the pop-up piece, (see Acute-angle V-fold, overleaf).

This pop-up spread is made with three Right-angle V-folds.

Acute-angle V-fold

The Acute-angle V-fold is the most common Foundation Shape. It folds down in the direction that the 'V' is pointing, so it can be placed at the top of a page, leaving plenty of room for text and additional illustrations.

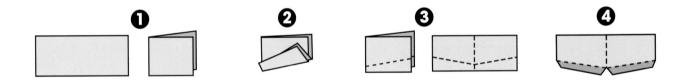

1 Fold the pop-up piece of card in half.

2 Fold an angled crease into it.

3 Open out the card.

4 Cut the bottom edge, below the angled crease, into gluing-tabs.

> ### GLUING
>
> The angles on the base – between the sticking strips and the spine – determine how this piece pops-up. Before gluing, look at the 'theory' box on the facing page and experiment with these angles.
>
> The gluing technique is the same as for the Right-angle V-fold, but in this case the mechanism is pointing forwards down the page (see 'Gluing' instructions on page 17).

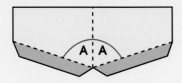

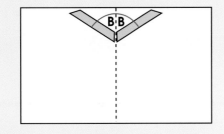

Above, angles **A** are the same as each other and bigger than angles **B** on the page.

Here, angles **B** match each other and must be less than 90˚.

Note the balance: the angles on the left, **A** + **B** = the angles on the right, **A** + **B**.

ADJUSTING THE ANGLE OF THE POP-UP PIECE

To make the pop-up piece stand more upright, make the angles on the page smaller, **A**, or the angles on the pop-up piece bigger, **B**.

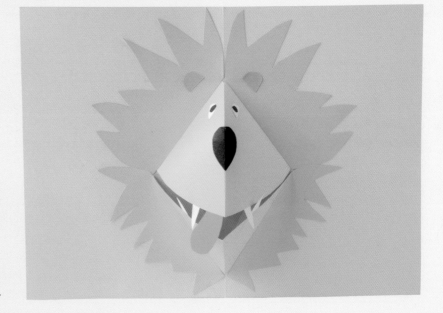

*With the base as a background, this type of V-fold is regularly used to create animal faces, with the V-fold 'jaws' jutting out forwards towards the viewer. The bigger the angles **B** on the page, the more the jaws will 'chomp'. In this case the bottom jaw is an Acute-angle V-fold, the top jaw a V-fold modified using 15.2 (see page 78).*

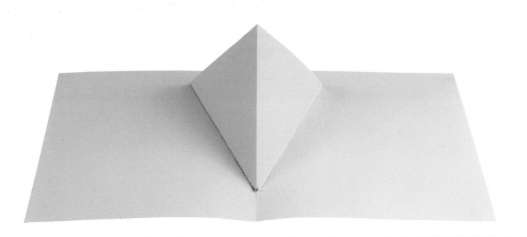

Pointed V-fold

This is the most simple V-fold. Easy to make and adapt, it is regularly used with the base as a vertical background. With the pointed end removed, it starts to look like a cross between a V-fold and a Parallelogram.

❶

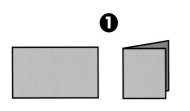

1 Fold the pop-up piece of card in half.

❷

 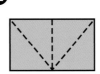

2 Fold a diagonal crease, from corner to corner, then unfold and open out.

❸

3 Cut the bottom edge, below the angled creases, into gluing-tabs.

GLUING

Follow the gluing method explained on page 17. Before gluing, experiment with the angles between the sticking strips and the spine.

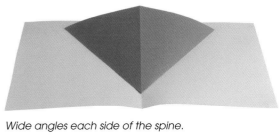

Wide angles each side of the spine.

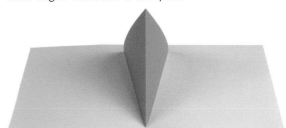

Narrow angles each side of the spine.

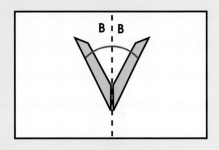

Angles **A** on the pop-up piece are bigger than angles **B** on the page.

All the creases converge at the same point on the spine line.

Note the balance: angles **A** + **B** on the left = the angles **A** + **B** on the right.

3.1 Creating gullies with the gluing-tabs

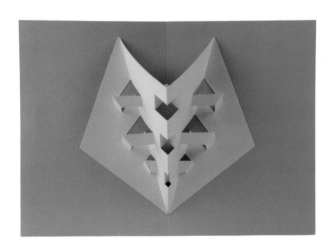

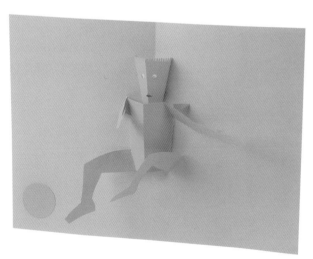

Here the outer edges are not tucked under the shape but come forward as part of the design. On this one the resulting gullies have Counter-folds cut into them (see page 108).

The head and body of this model are made with pointed V-folds with their ends removed. The arms and legs are glued onto small Counter-folds (see Building Techniques 5, page 108) built into the V-fold's gullies.

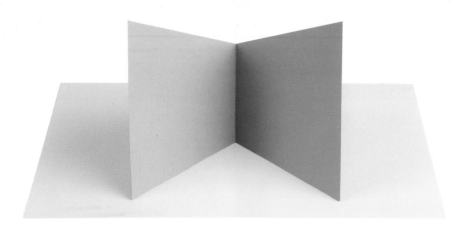

Obtuse-angle V-fold

The Obtuse-angle V-fold is probably the least common variant. Its main use is in combination with other shapes – most pop-up shapes need to be built into a gully, but this one works well built onto a Mountain-fold.

1 Fold the pop-up piece of card in half.

2 Fold an angled crease into it.

3 Unfold the card.

4 Cut the bottom edge, below the angled crease, into gluing-tabs.

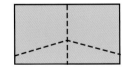

GLUING

1 Hold the piece on the base before gluing to check that the planned angles between the gluing-tabs and the spine are satisfactory.

2 Put glue on one tab and stick it to the page. Make sure the central fold on the pop-up is touching the spine.

3 Fold the pop-up piece into its closed position and put glue on the other tab.

4 Close the base and then press firmly.

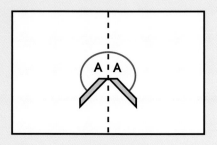

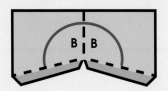

- Angles **A** must be bigger than angles **B**.

- If angles **A** are too small the piece won't sit on the page.

- The angles on the pop-up piece **B** are both more than 90°.

The Obtuse-angle V-fold can be used to straddle a Mountain-fold.

This simple Obtuse-angle V-fold demonstrates how large sections of a Foundation Shape can be cut away.

Asymmetric V-fold

The Asymmetric V-fold is a useful starting point for making interesting off-centre constructions. Although all the four angles on the base and pop-up piece are different, it still remains balanced on each side of the spine. Changing these angles produces remarkably different shapes.

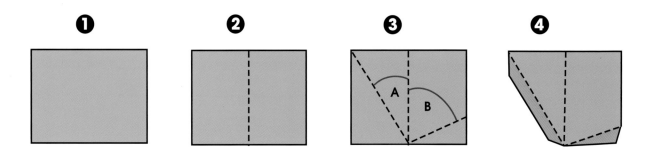

1 Start with approximately one third of a sheet of A4 card.

2 Fold a crease down the centre.

3 Fold two more creases, one on each side, meeting in a point at the bottom. Make sure that the angles (**A** and **B**) between these new creases and the central one are different.

4 Cut gluing-tabs below these creases.

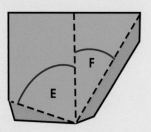

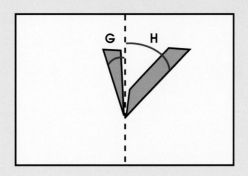

- All four angles are different.
- The two sides balance: angles on the left = angles on the right. **E** + **G** = **F** + **H**.
- Angles on the pop-up piece are bigger than the angles on the page. **E** + **F** is bigger than **G** + **H**.
- **F** is bigger than **G** by the same amount that **E** is bigger than **H**, i.e. **G** = 25°, **F** = 40°, **H** = 50°, **E** = 65°, (the angles on each side of the pop-up piece are 15° bigger than the angles on the page).

❺

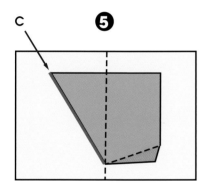

❻

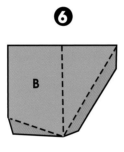

❼

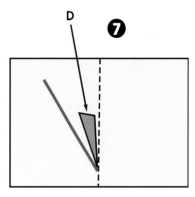

5 Place the piece flat on the base with the central crease flush with the spine fold.

With a pencil mark the line **C** where the crease of the small angle lies on the page.

6 Flip the pop-up piece over. The large angle on the pop-up piece **B** will go above the small angle marked on the page.

7 Glue the folded edge of the tab at a more acute angle **D** to the spine than the line marked on the page. Fold the pop-up piece into its closed position and put glue on the other tab. Close the base and press firmly.

Reference set of Asymmetric V-folds

Asymmetric pop-ups can make designs much more lively; however, without a reference set for guidance, the shapes produced can be fairly random. Here is a set of useful shapes. A protractor is necessary for constructing these.

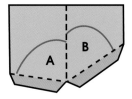

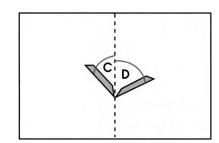

These two diagrams show the positions of the angles **A**, **B**, **C** and **D**, which are referred to in the photograph captions.

A = 85°, **B** = 60°, **C** = 50°, **D** = 75°

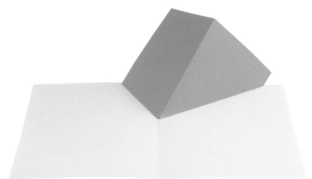

A = 75°, **B** = 45°, **C** = 30°, **D** = 60°

A = 90°, **B** = 60°, **C** = 30°, **D** = 60°

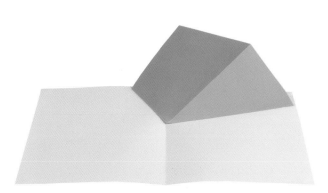

A = 85°, **B** = 35°, **C** = 30°, **D** = 80°

A = 120°, B = 50°, C = 10°, D = 80°

A = 95°, B = 45°, C = 25°, D = 75°

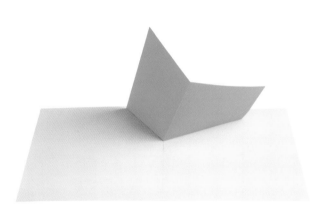

A = 105°, B = 75°, C = 30°, D = 60°

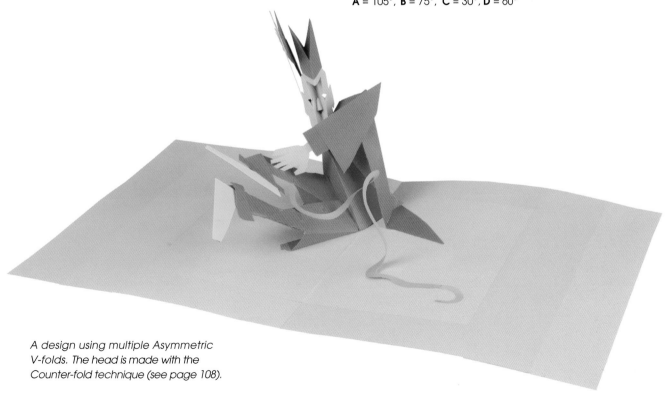

A design using multiple Asymmetric V-folds. The head is made with the Counter-fold technique (see page 108).

Parallel-folds

All the creases are parallel to the central gully of the base. This type of pop-up creates a stable ridge above the spine, which is good for building on.

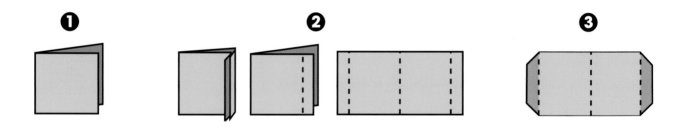

1 Fold the pop-up piece of card in half.

2 Fold over the ends parallel to the central crease, then open out.

3 Cut the gluing-tabs to shape.

4 Before gluing, experiment with the shape you want to create, for example try holding the gluing-tabs at different distances from the spine, close or further away.

GLUING

1 Glue one end to the base, parallel to the spine.

2 Fold the pop-up into its closed position. Put glue on the other tab.

3 Shut the base and press firmly (see also page 17).

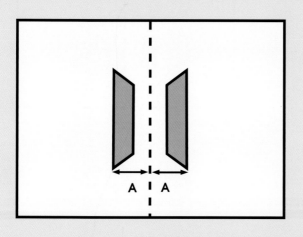 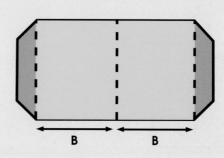

All the creases are parallel to the spine. Lengths **A** are shorter than **B**.

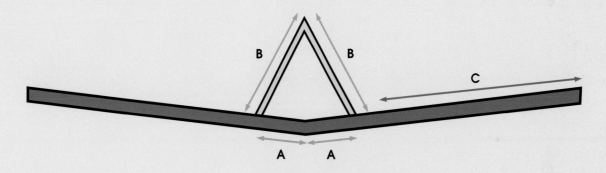

The lengths on each side balance: left side **A** + **B** = right side **A** + **B**.
Make sure that length **B** is less than **C**, or the pop-up will jut out from the base.

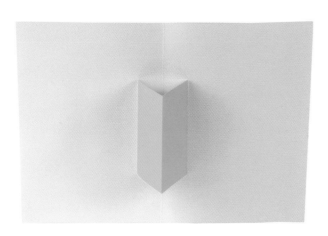

*This mechanism is commonly used
with the base as the background and
the pop-up coming forwards from it.*

6.1 Parallel-fold raising a plane instead of a ridge

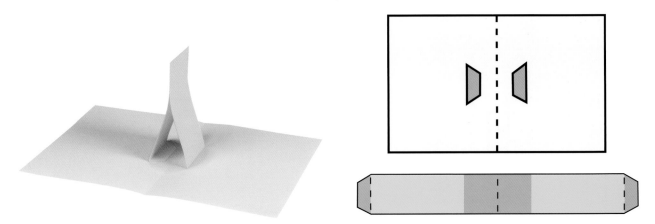

This simple variation is made with the two sides of the pop-up stuck together, back to back, instead of being folded. It's a useful way of raising a rigid plane above the spine.

This horse's body is made with a Parallel-fold, the head and tail are Angle-folded strips (see page 106) and the rider's body is a Curved variation of the Parallel-fold.

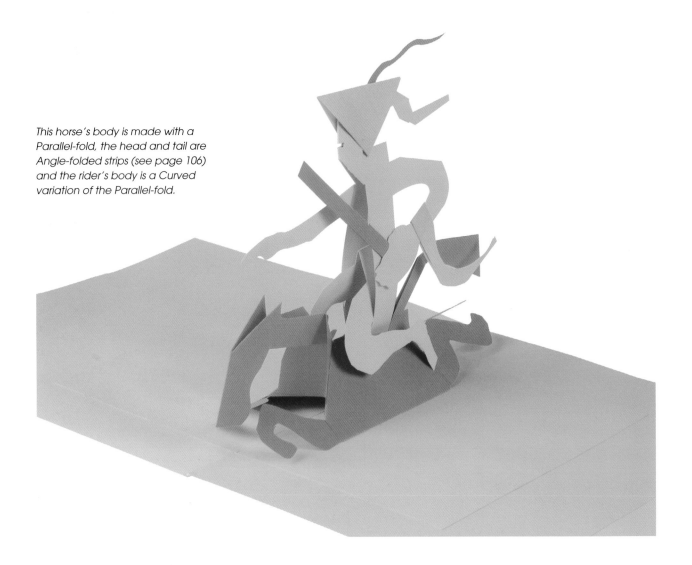

Curved variations with only one crease

These variations (6.2, 6.3 and 6.4, below) are fairly rare. They have only one fold in the middle of the pop-up piece, above and parallel to the spine-fold. Instead of having creases where they are glued to the page, they are glued flat, with the two ends flush up against the spine-fold. Although stable (they hold their shape when the base is open) they are not rigid, so are not suitable for raising large additional pop-ups.

6.2 Simple curve

6.3 Raising a plane

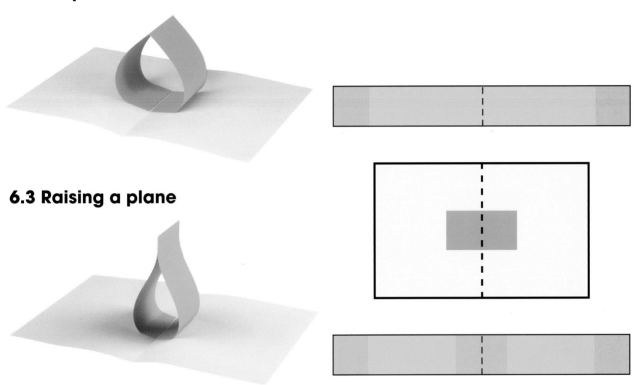

6.4 Asymmetric curve

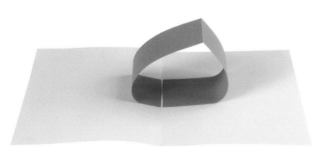

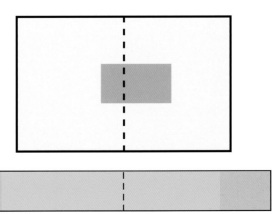

The single fold must be in the middle of the pop-up piece, and the two ends must be flush with the spine. Gluing different lengths of pop-up down on each end of the piece will create an asymmetric shape.

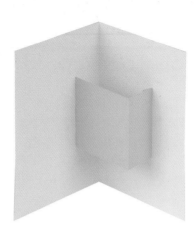

Foundation Shape 7

Parallelogram

The Parallelogram is unlike the other Foundation Shapes because, when the base is opened out flat, the Parallelogram lies flat. It is, however, a major pop-up 'building block'. It is used to create 'layers', either 'floating' parallel with the base, or else parallel with the supporting structure behind it. It is also the key mechanism in 'Moving arm' designs (see Foundation Shape 18, pages 88–93).

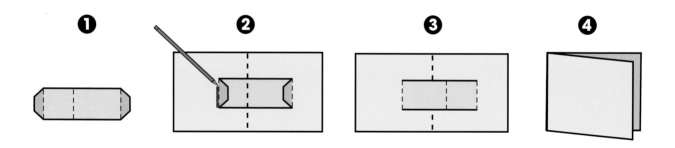

1 The Parallelogram has three parallel creases – one at each end where the gluing-tabs are attached, and a third which divides the whole piece into two different lengths.

2 Align the middle crease of the pop-up piece with the spine of the base.

On the page, mark the positions of the end creases of the pop-up piece.

3 Flip the pop-up piece round and glue the tabs to the marks. Both ends are glued with the base open flat and the pop-up piece flat. The crease on the long side of the pop-up piece glues to the short mark, and

the crease on the short side of the pop-up piece glues to the long mark.

4 Fold the base shut and press firmly to consolidate the gluing.

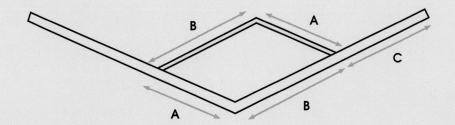

All the creases are parallel to the spine. Make sure that length **A** is shorter than length **C** or the pop-up will jut out from the base. The lengths on each side balance: on the left **A + B**, on the right, **B + A**.

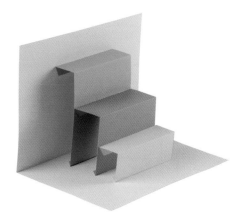

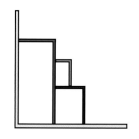

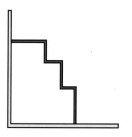

When the base-card is used like this, the design is commonly built purely out of Parallelograms.

This type of stepped structure has to be constructed with Parallelograms built upon Parallelograms.

Concertina-type structures are not stable and so do not work.

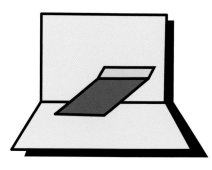

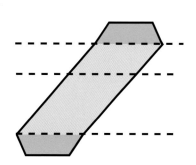

Although the Parallelogram's creases must be parallel, the edges of the pop-up piece can be any shape.

7.1 Building Parallelograms on to V-folds (type 1)

Using a V-fold to raise a Parallelogram is a very useful and easy-to-make combination. Here, the Parallelogram lifts as the base closes.

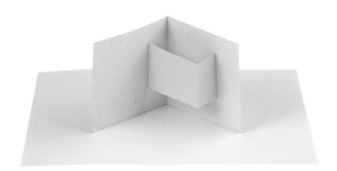

1 Start with a Right-angle V-fold. This can be constructed even if the V-fold is already mounted on the base.

2 Put the middle crease, **A**, of a Parallelogram tight into the middle gully of the V-fold.

3 On the V-fold, mark the positions of the end creases, **B** and **C**, of the Parallelogram.

4 Flip the Parallelogram round – glue the **B** tab to the **C** mark, and the **C** tab to the **B** mark.

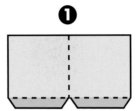

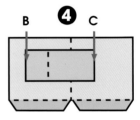

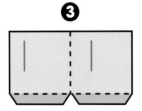

Multiple Parallelograms can produce intriguing, multi-layered effects. This whole construction will flatten out if the base is opened out flat.

7.2 Building Parallelograms on to V-folds (type 2)

On this type, the Parallelogram folds down as the base closes.

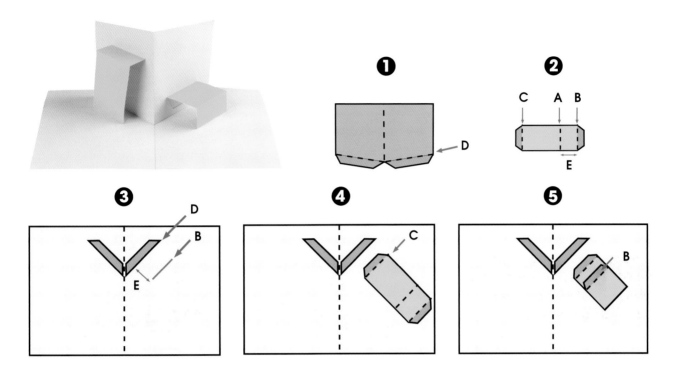

1 Start with an Acute-angle V-fold mounted on the base.

2 Make a Parallelogram piece.

3 Place the central fold of the Parallelogram, **A**, into the gully, **D**, formed where the V-fold is glued to the base. On the base mark the position of crease **B**. This method ensures that length **E** on the Parellogram is the same as length **E** on the base.

4 Flip the Parallelogram over and glue crease **C** to the mark.

5 Fold the Parallelogram into its closed (flat) position, put glue on tab **B** and close the base so that tab **B** finds its natural gluing position on the V-fold.

Parallelogram in action

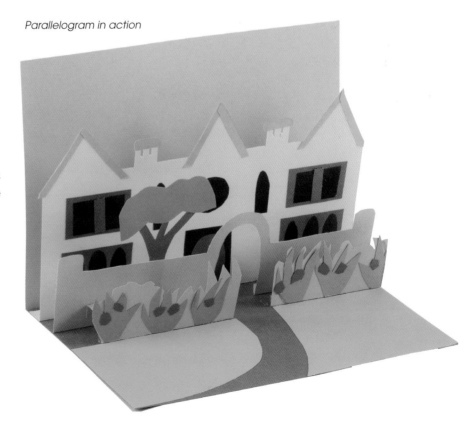

Foundation Shape 8

Asymmetric parallel-folds

This mechanism creates a stable, off-centre ridge above the page. It also produces contrasting gullies on each side of the base. When building complex pop-ups, it's a good alternative to the Parallelogram; whereas the Parallelogram can be used to raise planes parallel to other planes on the structure, this one can be used to introduce more variety.

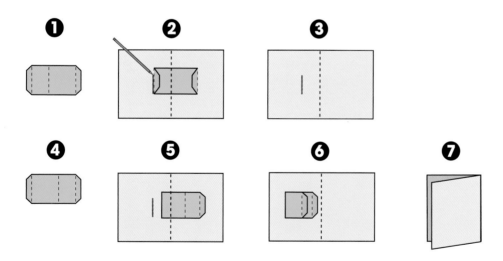

1 The sides of the pop-up piece are different lengths. All three creases are parallel.

2 Align the middle crease of the pop-up piece with the spine of the base.

3 On the page mark the position of the crease on the end of the short side.

4 Flip the pop-up piece over.

5 Glue the tab of the long side to the base, closer to the spine than the mark.

6 Fold the pop-up piece into its closed position and put glue on the other tab.

7 Close the base and then press firmly.

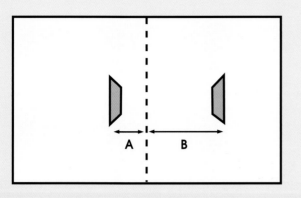 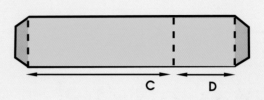

All the lengths are different. All the creases are parallel to the spine.

The lengths on each side balance:
$A + C = B + D$ (i.e. $A = 1$, $B = 2$, $C = 4$, $D = 3$). $C + D$ must be bigger than $A + B$.

This design is built with three Asymmetric parallel-folds. The lion is on a small one seen through a 'window' of a bigger one that is built over it. The third is built into the gully where the large one meets the base.

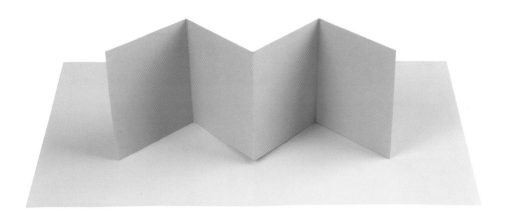

Foundation Shape 9

Zigzag-fold

This mechanism is based on the V-fold. It is easy to make, raises four planes and three gullies above the page as well as creating two gullies where it is attached to the page. These multiple planes and gullies give it great potential for building on.

❶

1 Make a fold along the bottom edge of a piece of card.

❷

2 Fold it in half.

3 With the piece folded in half, fold it in half again. Crease very thoroughly.

❸

4 Unfold the piece.

5 Remove the central sections below the long fold line and cut the gluing-tabs to shape at the base of the outer planes.

❹

❺

6

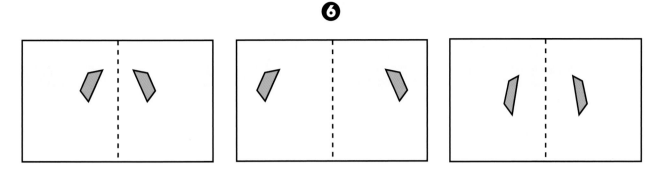

6 Before gluing, experiment with the shape of the piece on the page. The gluing-tabs need to be placed symmetrically on each side of the spine. However, their distance from the spine and their angle to the spine can all be varied and will give profoundly different results.

GLUING

1 Having decided on the desired shape, glue one side in position on the page.

2 Fold the pop-up piece down into its closed position, put glue on the other tab, shut the base and press firmly.

9.1 An alternative configuration of the pop-up piece

Angled secondary folds

The central fold should remain vertical and the two outer folds should mirror each other symmetrically. However, the two outer folds don't have to be vertical; by folding them at an angle you can start playing with the shape of the pop-up. The photographs below show the type of shape that can be produced using the configuration of folds shown in the diagrams.

9.2 Secondary folds angled upwards and inwards

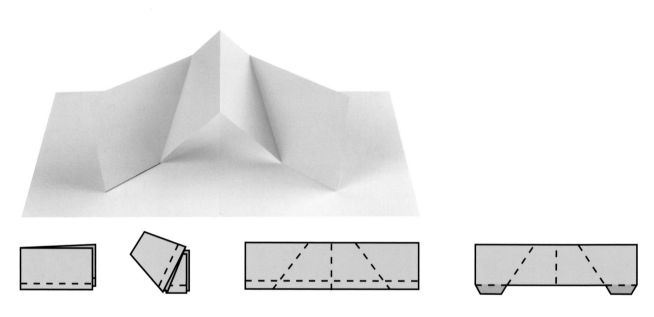

9.3 Secondary folds angled upwards and outwards

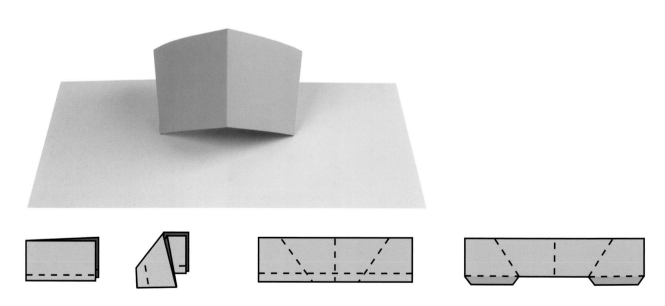

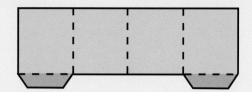
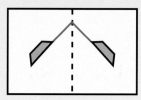

The most simple form of this mechanism is symmetrical, with three vertical creases. Its two sticking strips mirror each other and aim at the same point on the spine.

9.4 ASYMMETRIC VARIATION

This is a pleasing variation as it moves the central crease off to one side away from the spine. The sticking strips still aim at the same point on the spine. This is based on a V-fold raising a Parallelogram. When constructing it make sure the lengths balance as indicated in the diagram.

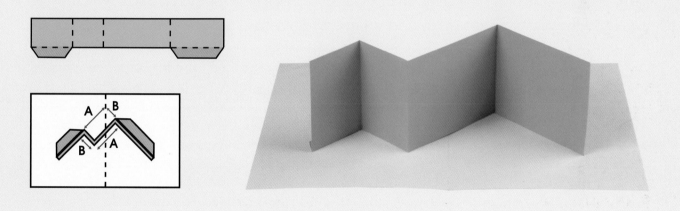

These houses are based on Parallelograms built into the vertical gullies of the Zigzag-fold. For this type of house see Project 1 (pages 142 and 146–147).

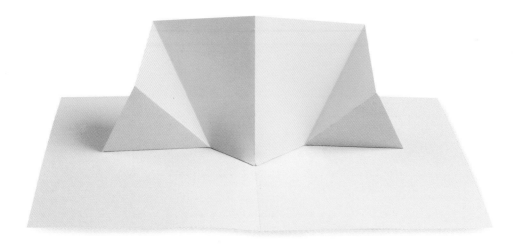

Foundation Shape 10

M-fold

This mechanism, made from one piece of card, is best understood as a triple V-fold. It is a very useful shape as it raises an array of six planes and nine gullies, all of which can be extended or used to raise additional pop-up shapes.

1 Take half a sheet of A4 card for the pop-up.

2 Fold the card in half.

3 Fold an angled crease in it.

4 Unfold the card and cut away a wedge from the centre – below the point where the three creases meet.

5 Fold up one of the sides.

6 With the side folded up, fold it again – this secondary fold (*) should be angled up and away from the central crease.

7 When the piece is folded out flat, these new creases should look like an arrow pointing towards (but not touching) the centre.

8 Repeat, making similar folds on the other half of the piece.

9 Cut four gluing-tabs below the fold lines at the bottom of the piece.

10 Thoroughly crimp each crease. On this version of the mechanism there are only two Valley-folds ('**V**'), one on each side of the central fold, all the others are Mountain-folds ('**M**').

11 To establish how they will lie when in the closed position, fold the whole piece into a concertina shape.

12 GLUING: follow the method used for Foundation Shape 2 (see page 32). Before gluing, experiment with the position on the page of the two central tabs,

tight in close to the spine, or further out at a wider angle. The different positions create very different shapes.

13 Start by gluing the central tabs. Glue side **A**, fold the pop-up piece into its closed position, put glue on tab **B** and shut the base so that tab **B** finds its correct symmetrical position.

14 Glue the two side tabs, one at a time. Fold tab **C** into its closed position, flat against the pop-up, apply glue, then fold the base shut so that tab **C** finds its natural position.

15 Repeat for tab **D**.

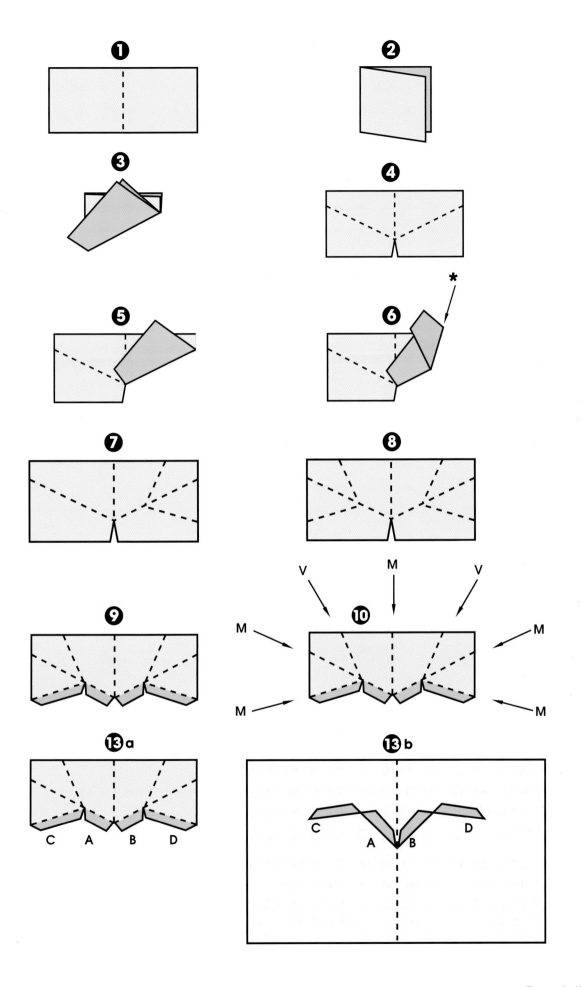

M-fold variations

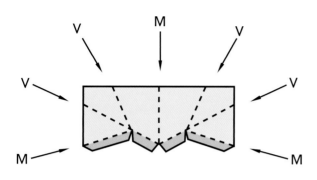

10.1

The two outer planes on each side of the mechanism can be configured to point backwards instead of forwards. In this case the four outer creases (two on each side of the central fold) are Valley folds.

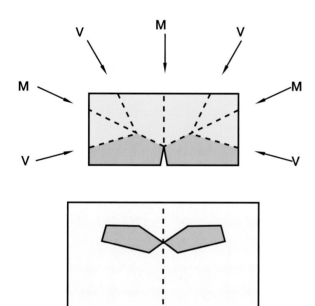

10.2

On this variation the bottom of the pop-up piece has not been cut to form four gluing-tabs which can be stuck down behind the body of the pop-up. Instead two large tabs are left, these have to come forward and glue to the base in front of the pop-up. This can be useful if Counter-folds (see pages 108–115) are being added to the front of the design.

10.3

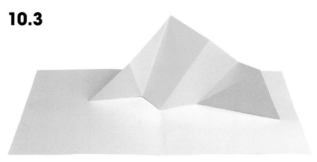

This variation uses an Asymmetric V-fold (see Foundation Shape 5, pages 38–41) to form the central body of the mechanism. The two sides are constructed as for shape 10 (see pages 56–57).

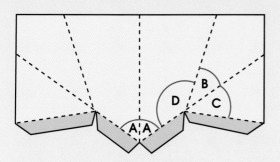

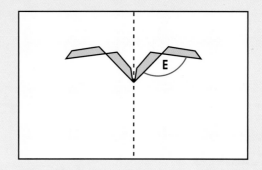

The most common formula for the angles on an M-fold is very straightforward:

A = A, B = C, D = E

The central angles **A** and **A** follow the rules that apply to V-folds (see Foundation Shapes 2 and 5, pages 32 and 38).

In all the examples illustrated here the outer angles **B** and **C** match, or mirror, each other. This is the most common form of the mechanism.

Usually, as in all these examples, angles **D** on the pop-up and **E** on the base are also the same as each other.

ADJUSTING THE ANGLES TO CHANGE THE SHAPE

Some designs break away from the basic symmetry – either to swing an outer pair of planes in towards the centre, or backwards away from it. This is the formula:

To swing the outer planes inwards:
Add the same amount (**x**) to both **B** and **D** so that they become bigger than **C** and **E**.
B = C + x, D = E + x, i.e. **B** = 70˚, **C** = 50˚, **D** = 130˚, **E** = 110˚, **x** = 20˚.

To swing the outer planes outwards, the formula is reversed. The same amount (**y**) is added to both **C** and **E** so they become bigger than **B** and **D**.
E = D + y, C = B + y, i.e. **E** = 130˚, **D** = 110˚, **B** = 60˚, **C** = 80˚, **y** = 20˚.

The central section of this M-fold is an Asymmetric V-fold; one of the two outer folds comes forwards, the other folds back.

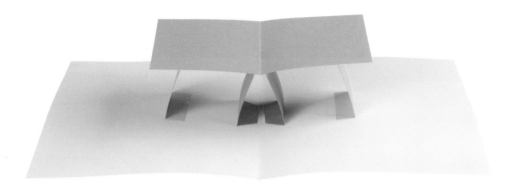

Floating plane

This mechanism, based on Parallel-folds, creates stable planes and a gully that 'float' above the page. It is often used with the base vertical, so that the planes float in front of the page. The array of hidden planes and gullies beneath the floating plane provide many opportunities for further extensions.

1 Make a fold up the middle of a piece of card.

2 With it folded in half, fold the outer edges to create gluing-flaps.

3 Unfold the card and cut it into three roughly equal pieces.

4 Glue one of the pieces onto the base to create a small Parallel-fold (Foundation Shape 6, page 42).

5 Use one of the small pieces to measure and mark, **A**, the sticking positions on the base on each side of the pop-up.

6 Glue the two remaining pieces, one on each side of the central pop-up, to create a pair of Parallelograms. The top creases of these two Parallelograms should be flush against the ridge of the Parallel-fold.

7 The Floating plane is made with another piece of card; it should be thoroughly creased and then glued on to the top of the two Parallelograms. Make sure that the crease on this piece is flush with the ridge above the spine.

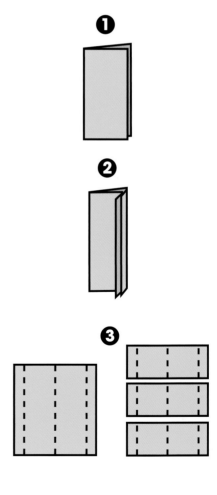

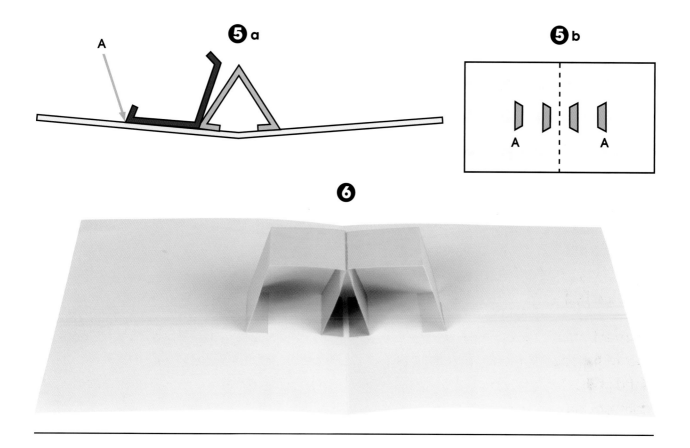

⑤a

⑤b

⑥

11.1 A wider Floating plane

1 If a very wide floating layer is desired, the Parallelograms can be constructed using small supports further away from the spine. In this case, make sure that these supports are the same height **B** as the central Parallel-fold and that the sticking distance on the base **C** matches the length on the underside of the Floating plane.

2 When building this wider Floating plane the central support (Parallel-fold) can have a small gluing-flap cut into one side of it – this glues to the underside of the Floating plane flush with its central crease.

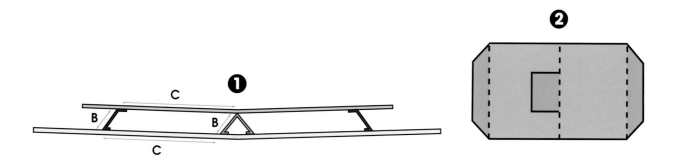

❶

❷

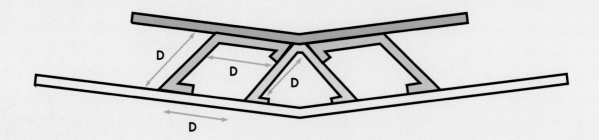

The Parallel-fold (Foundation Shape 6, page 42) creates a stable ridge in the middle. This supports two Parallelograms (Foundation Shape 7, page 46), one on each side. Lengths **D** are all the same.

ASYMMETRIC VARIATIONS

11.2 An Asymmetric parallel-fold (Foundation Shape 8, see page 50) can be used as the central support – this moves the floating gully off-centre. Building two Parallelograms (Foundation Shape 7, see page 46) on each side of it keeps the Floating plane parallel with the base.

11.3 Alternatively, Asymmetric parallel-folds (Foundation Shape 8, page 50) can be built on each side of the central support to change the angles of the Floating planes.

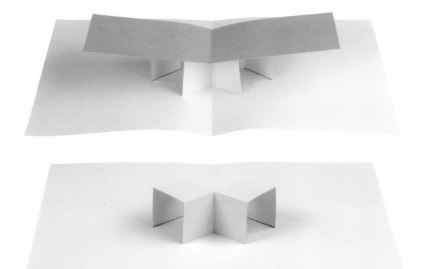

11.4 Floating planes based on a V-fold

For this, a Right-angle V-fold (see Foundation Shape 1, page 30) is used instead of a Parallel-fold to provide the central support. The V-fold raises a pair of Parallelograms. This variation folds down in another way, which gives it a different action, as the base opens and closes.

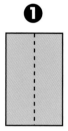 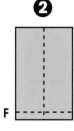 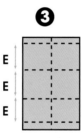  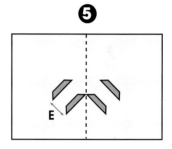

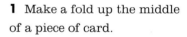

1 Make a fold up the middle of a piece of card.

2 Make another crease **F**, for gluing-tabs, ½in (13mm) above the bottom edge.

3 Use the width of the ruler **E** to score three more, equidistant, parallel lines.

4 Cut between the two sides as shown. Cut gluing-tabs onto the ends.

5 First stick the V-fold section that straddles the spine.

The other ends stick to the base with the crease a ruler's width behind the V-fold.

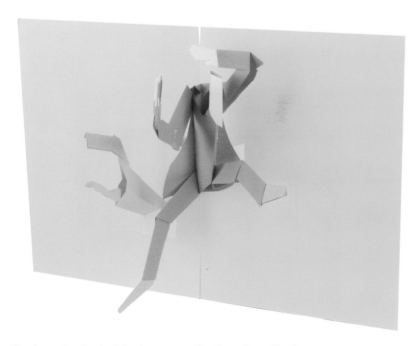

The figure is raised off the base on a Floating plane. The torso is a Parallel-fold, the limbs are made with Angle-folded strips.

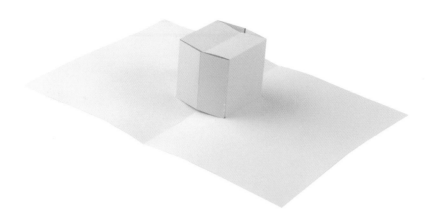

Foundation Shape 12

Box

This highly adaptable mechanism is the basis of many solid, sculptural pop-ups. The example explained here is a simple cubic Box which is constructed using only four pieces of card. This is one of the few Foundation Shapes that needs measuring and drawing out, however – in this simple form – the measuring is very easy.

1 This Box is made with four pieces of card, two identical pieces of **1a** and two of **1b**.

2 There are only two measurements: **A** = one unit, and **B** = 2 x **A**. Try making **A** equal the width of a ruler.

3 Draw, score, and cut out the four pieces. Crease the folds thoroughly.

4 Glue tabs **C** to the base; planes **D** should rise from the spine-fold.

5 Glue planes **D** back to back – this part of the mechanism pushes the whole construction into shape; making it double thickness like this prevents it from buckling.

6 Draw guidelines **E** onto the base parallel to the spine.

7 Glue tabs **E** to the base. At this point the structure consists of two Parallelograms, back to back, centred on the spine. This is an unstable shape which wobbles from side to side and may not pop-up when the spread is opened.

8 Glue tabs **F**. These are the ends of the Box, which link the two outer planes and turn the construction into a rigid pop-up shape when the page is open.

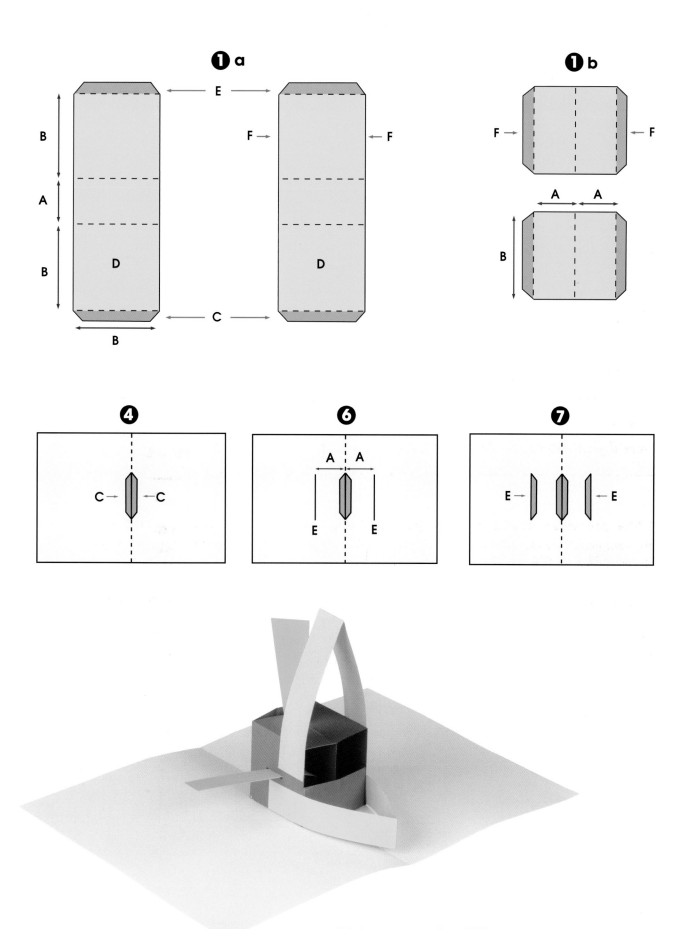

1 a

B
A
B
D
B
E
C

F
F
D

1 b

F
F

A
A

B

4

C → ← C

6

A
A
E
E

7

E →
← E

This shows a range of possibilities that can be added to a Box.

Two identical Parallelograms, back to back, are centred on the spine fold.

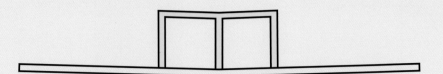

As the base opens, the central plane rises and pushes up the lid and this in turn pushes out the top of the sides. An end piece, attached to the two outer planes, 'locks' the mechanism upright when the page is open. These three components – the central pillar, the lid and the end piece – are all vital to this mechanism.

Parallel-folds and other structures can be built on top of the box. However, the box must always have the pillar and 'lid' structure, whether or not it is visible.

The end piece does not have to be the full height of the structure, or even shaped to form a square end. Whatever its size or shape there must be a piece joining the two outer sides.

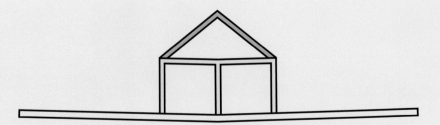

12.1 Cylindrical Box

The Box can be modified into a cylinder. To make this, combine the circular shape that can be produced with Foundation Shape 13 (page 68) with the central pillar and lid essential to this Box mechanism. The lid on this type of Box has to be cut to shape on the model.

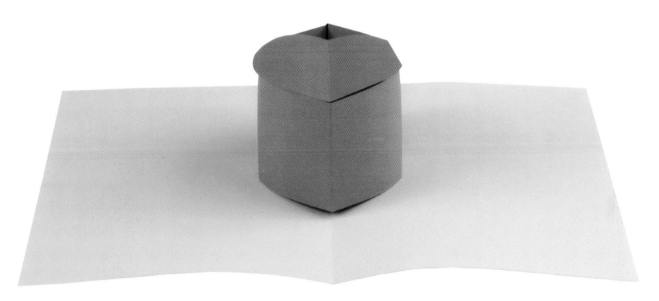

The Box provides the underlying structure for this model. The figures inside are made with an Obtuse-angle V-fold glued to the lid of the Box. The bonnet, windscreen and roof are all modified Parallel-folds added to the top of the Box.

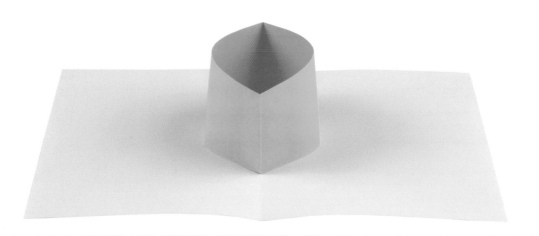

Foundation Shape 13

Open-topped shapes

This shape is made with a simple loop of card. It has four gullies that can be used for building onto – one on each side where it is attached to the base, and one at each end – rising up above the spine.

1 Make a strip of card approximately 2in (50mm) wide. Fold a crease along its length ½in (13mm) above the bottom edge. Fold another crease ½in (13mm) in from one end – this one is the gluing-tab that will glue the strip into a loop.

2 Fold the remainder of the strip in half.

3 With the strip still folded, cut away the bottom edge leaving a gluing-tab approximately 1in (25mm) long in the middle of each side.

4 Unfold the strip and crimp all the folds.

5 Glue the strip into a loop. Make sure the loop can flatten out.

6 Before gluing the piece in place, experiment with the shape on the base. The creases at each end should both be directly above the spine. The two gluing-tabs must both be parallel to, and the same distance from, the spine. However, they may be close to the spine, creating a long narrow shape, or further away from it, creating an approximate circle.

7 Stick one tab to the page, parallel with the spine.

8 Fold the loop down into its closed position lying flat against the page.

9 Put glue on the other tab.

10 Close the base and then press firmly.

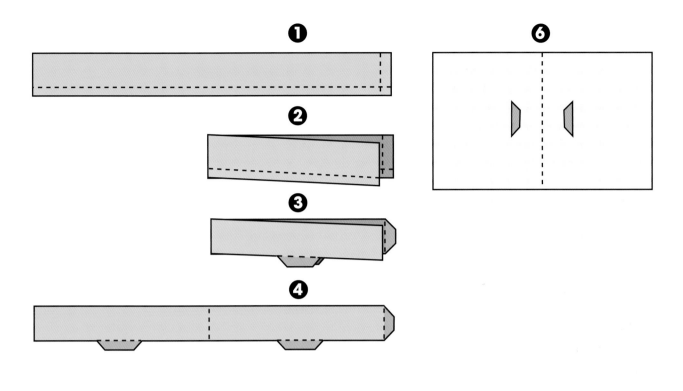

13.1 Open-topped square

The most simple variation is to add extra vertical creases to give the shape corners. This shape cannot be made too tall or, due to the bendiness of card, the 'walls' will not remain vertical and will tend to lean in towards the centre.

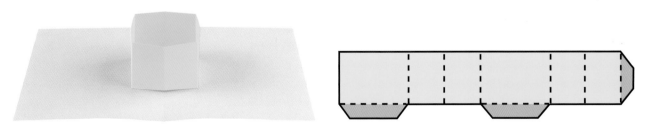

Adding extra vertical creases changes the pop-up into a rectangle. The base layout remains the same.

13.2 and 13.3 Tapered variations

To pull the top of the shape in, or splay it out, the strip that the piece is made of needs to be curved. In these examples the two shapes are based on semicircles – a more gentle curve will produce a similar but less severe result. The only crucial creases are the ones marked **A** and **B**, which will be above the spine, allowing the shape to fold flat. The other creases are not vital, their effect is to break the shape down into facets rather than leaving it as a curve.

Constructing these tapered shapes

Use a compass to draw two concentric arcs. Then use it to measure out six equal lengths on one of them. All the fold lines go from these points to the centre of the circles. The gluing method is the same as for the previous versions of this mechanism, with the gluing-tabs attached to the base, parallel to the spine.

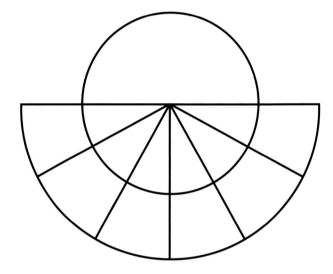

13.2

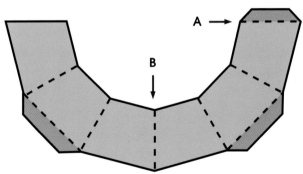

13.3

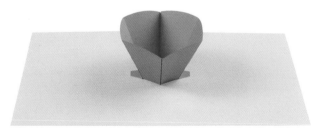

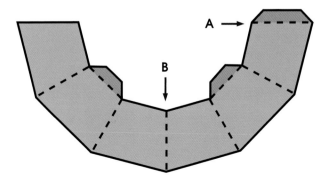

13.4 Open-topped shapes on a V-fold

An alternative format for this shape is to construct the gluing-tabs next to each other and attach them to the base like a V-fold instead of a Parallel-fold.

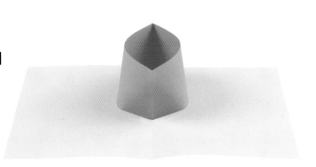

The first two steps of construction are identical to those on page 68.

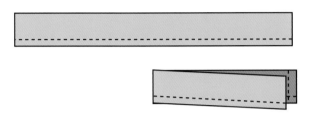

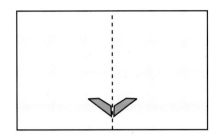

The gluing method is the same as for V-folds (see page 17).

In this case, though, the two gluing-tabs go one on each side of one of the end creases.

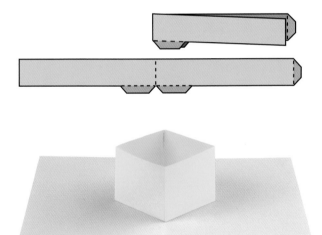

13.5 Rectangular variation

The V-fold version can also have added vertical creases – these convert the loop into a Parallelogram.

This boat is based on Foundation Shape 13.3 and the figure is based on Building Technique 3 (see page 102).

Pyramids

This is probably the easiest solid pop-up shape to construct. Its shape can vary from tall, narrow and pointy to low and squat. It is also very rigid, so large parts can be cut away without it losing its shape.

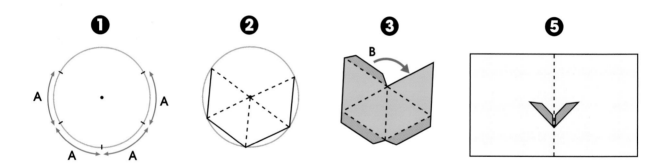

Constructing the Pyramid

1 Draw a circle – its centre will be the apex of the Pyramid. Use a compass to measure out equal lengths, **A**, around the circumference.

2 Score from these points to the centre.

3 Add two tabs on adjacent sides to stick it to the base. Add a tab, **B**, to pull the whole piece into shape. Score the creases where the three gluing-tabs are attached.

4 Glue the tab that pulls it into shape first. When glued, make sure that the whole piece will fold flat.

5 Glue the piece to the base using the same method as for V-folds (see page 17).

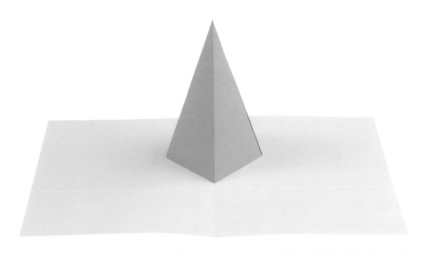

A tall, thin Pyramid: making the sides at the base of the Pyramid short in relation to its height will create a steep, narrow Pyramid.

Pyramid variations

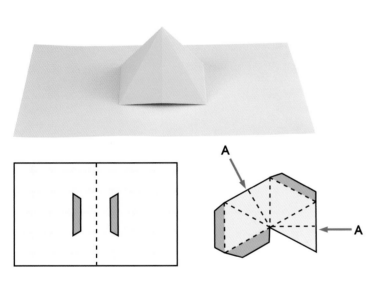

14.1 Parallel-fold Pyramid

This type of Pyramid is based on Parallel-folds. The two gluing-tabs that attach it to the base lie parallel to the spine and are built onto opposite outer edges. This type of Pyramid needs two extra creases, **A** and **A**, in the centre of the planes above the gully.

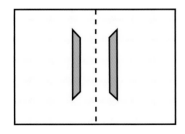
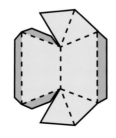

14.2 Elongated Pyramid

This shape is based on the Parallel-fold (Foundation Shape 6, page 42) with half a Pyramid added to each end. When making this the bottom edges of the ends will need to be 'tailored' to fit the page.

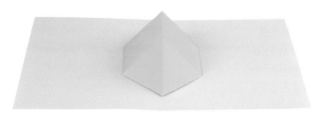

14.3 Asymmetric Pyramid

This type of Pyramid is based on the Asymmetric V-fold.

1 Draw a circle. Use a compass to measure off lengths around the circumference: short **A** – long **B** – short **A** – long **B**. The top of the pyramid is the centre of the circle. Score from the outer points to the centre.

2 Add two gluing-tabs on adjacent outer sides to stick the piece to the base. Add a tab, **E**, to pull the whole piece into shape. Measure the two angles **C** and **D**.

3 Since this Pyramid is not square, the gluing positions on the base have to be calculated.

The formula is:
Angle **C** is a bigger angle than **D**.
C – **D** = **H**.
(**H** is the difference between **C** and **D**.)
On the base angle **G** is a bigger angle than **F**.
G + **F** = 90°.
F = 45° – ½ **H**.
G = 45° + ½ **H**.
(e.g. **C** = 70°, **D** = 40°, **H** = 30°,
F = 45° – 15° = 30°, **G** = 45° + 15° = 60°.)
C goes over **F**, **D** goes over **G**.

14.4 The Cone

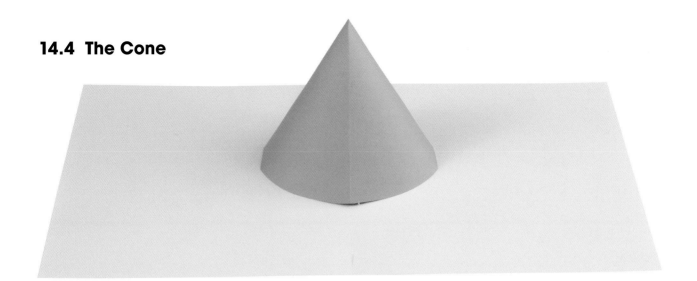

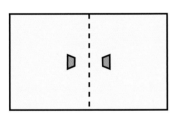

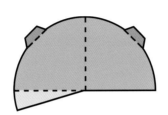

The most simple of the Pyramid variations – the two tabs that attach the cone to the page should be very short, in relation to the height of the cone.

The camel is based on the Asymmetric pyramid, with large parts cut away. The head and neck are made with an Angle-folded strip (see Building Technique 4.3, page 107).

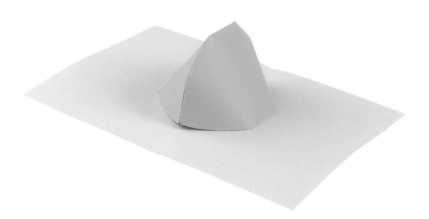

Foundation Shape 15

Curved shapes

Curved folds are created by breaking the curve down into a series of short, straight, sections. The principle can be applied to both Parallel-folds and V-folds. It can be used to create a large, bulbous shape, or used on a predominantly straight piece to make it bend.

1 Fold a piece of card in half.

2 Fold up a ½in (13mm) strip along the outer edges to create gluing-tabs.

3 Leave a gluing-tab in the middle of each side and trim away the rest of the card below the folded line.

4 Draw two guide lines running from points **A** to points **B**. These will be the curves, which need to be made up of a series of short straight lines. In this case, each side is made up of two straight sections, but for an even smoother curve it could be three sections or even four.
Points A: Leave a gap between points **A**, the hinge of the whole piece. In this example, its length

and position roughly matches the gluing-tabs.

Points B: Positioned above the corners, these are approximately three-quarters of the way down the side of the folded card. The curved line doesn't come right down to the corner, or the pop-up piece won't fit neatly against the base – see step 11 (facing page).

5 Follow the guide lines and cut away the top corners from the top layer of card. On the bottom layer, leave the top corners in place.

6 Use the top half of the card as a guide, and draw along the cut edges of the short straight lines to create a mirror image on the bottom layer.

7 Unfold the card.

8 Draw, cut and fold gluing-tabs, **C**, onto the guide lines drawn on the bottom layer.

9 Fold the gluing-tabs **C** inwards. Glue the two sides together to create a pocket – the piece should fold flat. Ensure that the glue hasn't oozed and that the 'pocket' can open freely.

10 The tabs, **D**, glue down parallel to the spine. Before gluing the piece to the base, experiment with the best distance between the tabs and the spine: the further away from the spine they are, the more globular the pop-up shape.

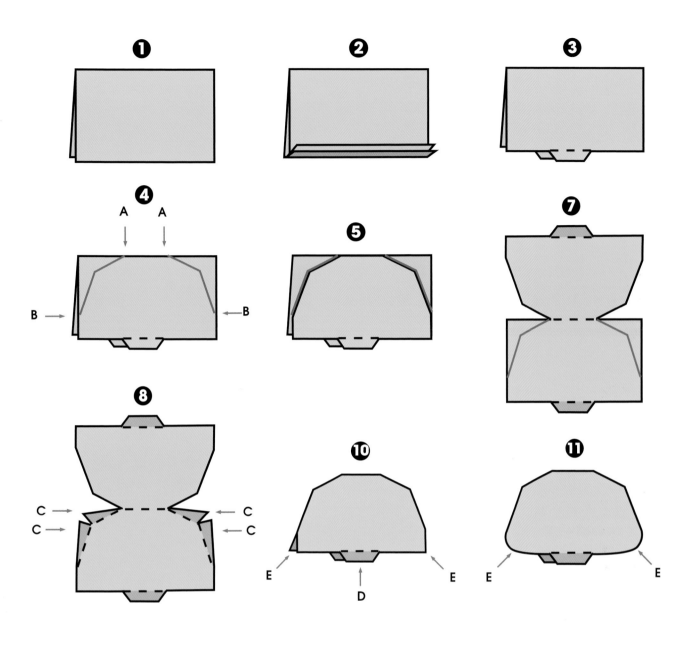

11 Before gluing, the bottom corners, **E**, need to be trimmed to fit neatly against the page. The amount to be cut away will depend on how bulbous the pop-up shape is.

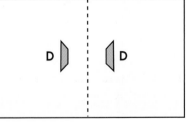

This is a sturdy shape – large parts can be cut away and the pop-up will still work well.

GLUING

Glue one side down first, then fold the whole piece into its closed position, flat against the base; put glue on the other tab; close the base and press firmly.

15.1 Curved shapes based on V-folds

The shape can be constructed as a V-fold and, although it looks very similar, it will fold away differently as the base closes. In this case the tabs that fix the shape to the base have to be moved from the middle of the outer edges to the corners, tabs **G**.

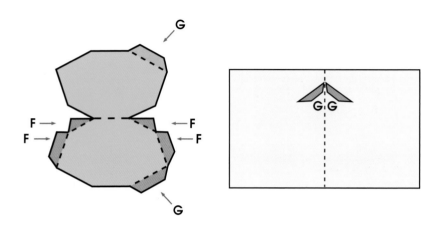

15.2 Simple Curved shape based on a V-fold

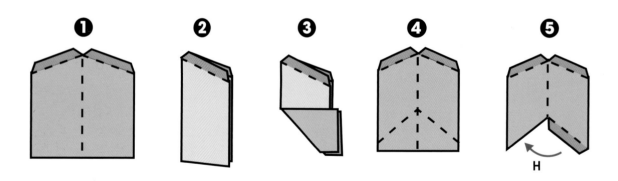

1 Make an Acute-angle V-fold (see page 32).

2 Fold it in half.

3 With the piece folded in half add an angled crease.

4 Unfold the piece.

5 Cut away one of the little triangles and trim the other into a gluing-tab.

6 Stick this tab, **H**, first. Ensure that the piece will fold flat.

7 Glue the piece to the base using the same method as for Foundation Shape 2 (see page 32). Before gluing, experiment with the angles between the tabs and the spine – the bigger the angle **G** between the gluing-tabs and the spine, the more the piece will move as the base closes.

15.3 Adding creases to a curve

These shapes can be further refined by adding extra creases, which will turn the curved plane into a series of facets.

❶ 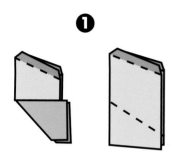 **❷**  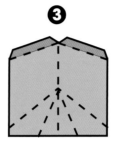 **❸** 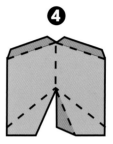 **❹**

1 Start with step 3 from the previous variation.

2 Add another smaller angled crease.

3 Open out, and make sure all the creases meet at the same point.

4 Cut away one little triangle. Cut the other triangle into a gluing-tab.

This Curved shape is based on the V-fold variation. The ears are formed from the gluing-tabs that attach the piece to the base.

A range of possibilities that can be added to a Curved shape.

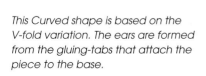

Foundation Shape 16

Twisting mechanism

This mechanism produces an intriguing twisting action as the page opens. It has six planes, which can be extended, and seven gullies to build into.

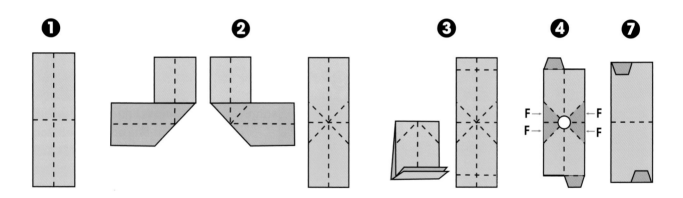

1 Fold the piece in half – both ways.

2 Using the central folds as guides, fold two diagonal creases meeting at the centre. Eight angles are being created here, all of them 45°. (Some people find it easier to draw them up with a protractor, rather than using this folding method.)

3 Fold the piece in half, then fold over the ends to make the gluing-tabs.

4 Cut the two gluing-tabs to shape. There is one at each end, diagonally opposite each other.

5 To reduce thickness, remove a small piece from the centre, where the creases converge.

6 Glue the piece to the base. It should be opened out flat with the long central fold aligned with the spine. Apply glue to the small triangles **F**.

7 The top piece must not be shorter than the piece that is glued to the base. It is glued onto the two end flaps with its central fold at right angles to the spine.

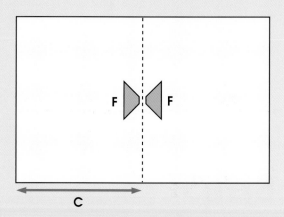

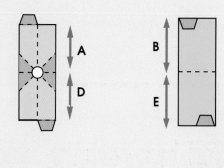

- This mechanism is made up of two opposing V-folds which, in essence, are raising a Parallel-fold.

- Lengths **A** + **B** must be less than length **C**.

- **B** + **E** must be the same or longer than **A** + **D**.

- The creases on each side of the central fold are all 45˚.

The quadrilateral can be built asymmetric.
A + **B** = **D** + **E**.

Twisting mechanism in action.

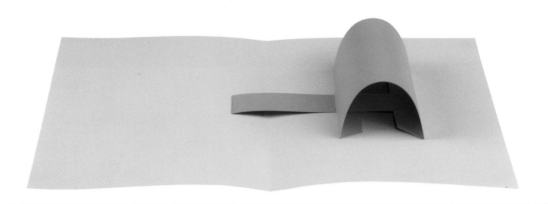

Foundation Shape 17

Automatic pull-strip

This mechanism uses a strip of card spanning the spine to raise a pop-up on the opposite page. The pop-up can be a Curved shape (as here), a flap, or a Parallelogram. The strip can be concealed beneath the page, which makes the effect even more surprising.

1 First, take a piece of card approximately 4in (100mm) wide and 10in (254mm) long. Make folds for gluing-tabs at each end, and a third parallel fold about 1in (25mm) off centre. Length **A** plus one gluing-tab should be slightly less than one side of your card base. Length **A** should be longer than length **B**.

2 Use the width of a ruler to draw two horizontal, parallel guide lines (**C** and **C**).

3 Draw the rest of the shape. The edges of tab **D** lie just within the guide lines. The edges of tabs **E** are just outside the guide lines.

4 Cut out the piece. The shape **F** to the left of the middle fold is an integral part of the strip; it guides the moving edge that slides on the page as the base opens.

5 Crease all the folds.

6 Fold the main body of the piece over the strip.

7 Fold tabs **E** underneath it.

8 Place the piece on the base with crease **G** not more than 1in (25mm) away from the spine.

9 Before gluing, try pulling tab **D**, to make sure that the strip can slide freely between tabs **E**.

10 With the whole piece in position, flat on the page, glue tabs **E**.

11 Leave tab **D** flat on the page (NOT folded). Put glue on top of tab **D**, then close the base. Allow the glue to set before opening as tab **D** takes a lot of stress when the base is opened.

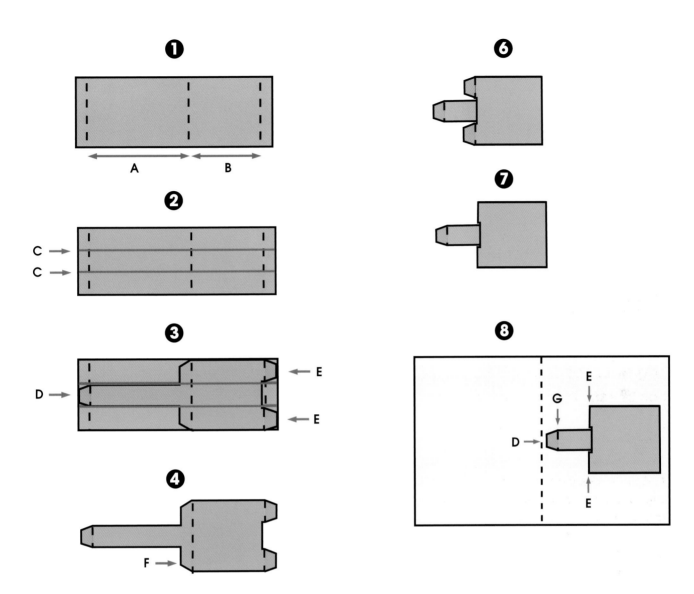

❶

A   B

❷

C →
C →

❸

D →
E
E

❹

F →

❻

❼

❽

E
G
D →
E

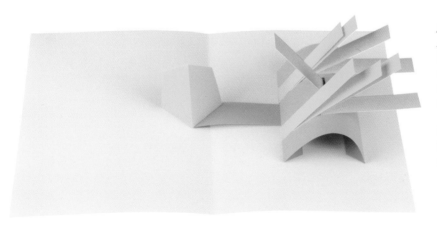

Additions

Additional flat strips can be added to this curved shape. Put glue on the end of the strips – they will rise at different angles, depending on where they are attached to the curve.

Other pop-ups can also be built into the little gully created where the strip attaches to the base.

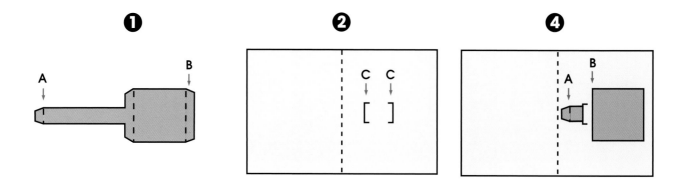

17.1 Running the Automatic pull-strip under the page

The strip can be constructed to run under the base. This holds the sliding part of the mechanism down on the page, it also hides the pull-strip and gets it out of the way of other pop-up constructions.

1 In this variation the end of the pull-strip near the spine, **A**, is exactly the same as in the previous example, but the construction at the other end is slightly different – it has one long gluing-tab, **B**, all the way across the width of the piece.

2 Two slits are cut in the base, **C** and **C**. Note the shape of these slits – their ends are extended horizontally by about ½in (13mm) to allow the page to lift slightly, and so facilitate the movement of the card.

3 Construction: the strip is threaded through the slits until crease **A** is approximately ½in (13mm) from the spine; leave the gluing-tab lying flat.

4 Fold the body of the card over towards the spine and fold tab **B** underneath it.

5 With the piece lying flat, glue tab **B** to the page between the two slits.

6 Put glue on top of tab **A**, then close the base and press firmly. Give the glue time to set before opening the page.

Here an automatic pull-strip running under the page is used to raise an array of Parallelograms. The images are glued to the top surfaces of the Parallelograms.

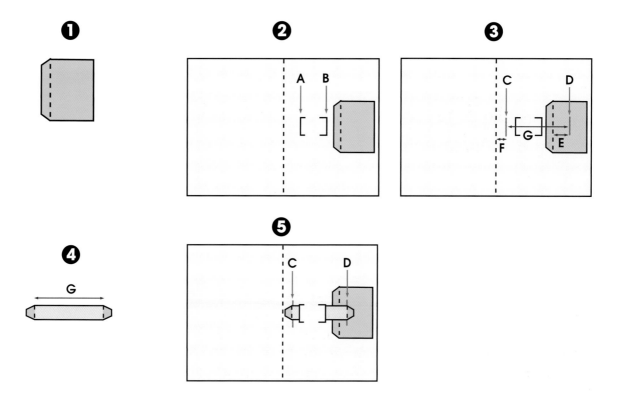

17.2 Using the Automatic pull-strip to raise a flap in the middle of the page

1 Make the flap – a piece of card with a gluing-tab on one side.

2 Glue the flap to the page. Make two slits in the page – be sure to leave enough of a gap between slit **A** and the spine, and slit **B** and the flap for the pull-strip to be able to move comfortably.

3 Draw a line, **C**, on the page parallel to the spine and about ½in (13mm) away from it. Draw a line, **D**, on the flap parallel to the crease where the flap is attached to the page. One end of the pull-strip will be attached here. The position of this line, **D**, is critical. To make the flap flip right over make length **E** = length **F**. To make the flap stand vertical make **E** = 2 x **F**. Measure the distance between the two lines, **G**.

4 Make the pull-strip with a gluing-tab at each end. The distance between the gluing-tabs' creases is **G**.

5 Thread the pull-strip through the slots in the base.

Glue one end of the pull-strip to the flap with the gluing-tab's crease exactly on line **D**.

Make sure the crease at the other end of the strip is exactly on line **C** then, with the gluing-tab flat, put glue on the top of it, shut the base and press firmly.

1 With the base closed this is the position of crease **A** in relation to the spine.

2 With the base open, crease **A** moves to position **B** in relation to the spine. The distance between position **A** and position **B** is the amount of movement generated at the other end of the strip, **C**.

At its most simple, this movement can be used to pull a flat image across the page. It can also be used to flip a flap, or raise a plane which can in turn lift Parallelograms or V-folds. (For measurements when raising or flipping flaps see 17.2, step 3, on page 85.)

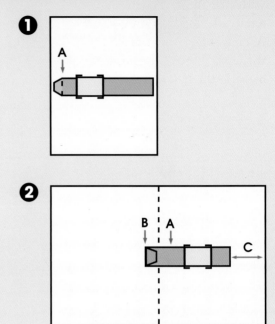

17.3 A Parallelogram can be built onto the flap rising in the middle of the page

1 Make a flap rise on the page as explained in 17.2 (see page 85). In this case at step 3, **E** will be 2 x **F**.

2 Make a Parallelogram piece – length **A** will be the same height as the raised flap.

3 Length **B** on the Parallelogram will be the same as the distance between the place where the flap's crease is fixed to the page and where the Parallelogram glues down between the two slits in the base.

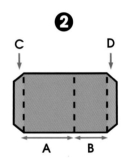

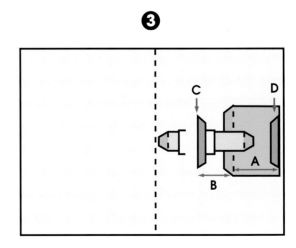

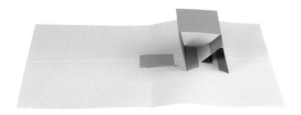

17.4 Automatic pull-strip turning a flap on the opposite page

1 This mechanism is made with two pieces. The first is a pull-strip with a gluing-tab, **A**, on one end and a flap on the other. There is a fold, **B**, between the flap and the strip.

2 The second piece is a rectangle of card with a gluing-tab, **C**, in the middle of one edge. There is a crease between the gluing-tab and the card. Tab **C** will glue to the back of the flap. The other edge of the card, **D**, will glue down flat and flush against the edge of the base.

3 Place the strip with **A** opened out flat and almost touching the spine of the base. Fold the flap over on top of the strip. Distance **E** between the spine and the crease of flap **A** must be the same as **E** between crease **B** and the crease of flap **C**.

4 Glue the second piece into position with edge **D** flush against the edge of the page and tab **C** glued to the back of the flap.

5 Put glue on top of flap **A**. Close the base, press firmly and allow the glue on tab **A** to set.

6 Open the base. Because the flap is folding towards the closing page it may need to be trimmed, as it will snag if it is too long.

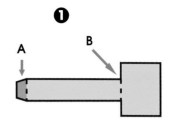

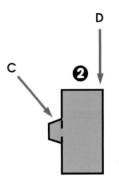

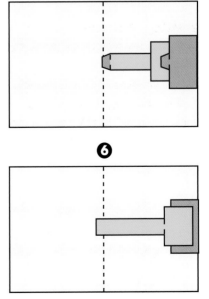

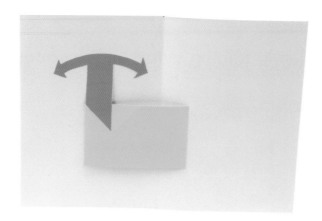

Foundation Shape 18

Moving arms

These subtle mechanisms, which make 'arms' move as the page opens, are excellent for adding dynamic action to a design. To give the arm maximum movement, these are usually based on mechanisms which flatten out when the base is opened out. The size and shape of the moving piece can vary enormously – it may be the whole body of a figure, rather than just its arm.

Arms powered by a Parallelogram

The most common variants of this mechanism are made with small, double-triangles folded into the gullies formed by a Parallelogram. The moving 'arm' is glued to one of these small triangles, and the position of the triangle dictates the direction and type of movement of the 'arm'.

Start as though making a Parallelogram (see Foundation Shape 7, page 46).

1 Take a piece of card.

2 Fold a gluing-tab onto each end.

3 Fold a third parallel crease slightly less than 1in (25mm) away from one of the gluing-tabs.

4 Fold over the top corner.

5 Fold over the bottom corner.

6 Unfold. This is the basic Parallelogram with the addition of two small triangles folded into both the top and bottom of the middle fold.

7 With the base flat, glue the piece to the base.

8 The moving arms glue to any, or all, of the little triangles, **E**, **F**, **G** and **H**.

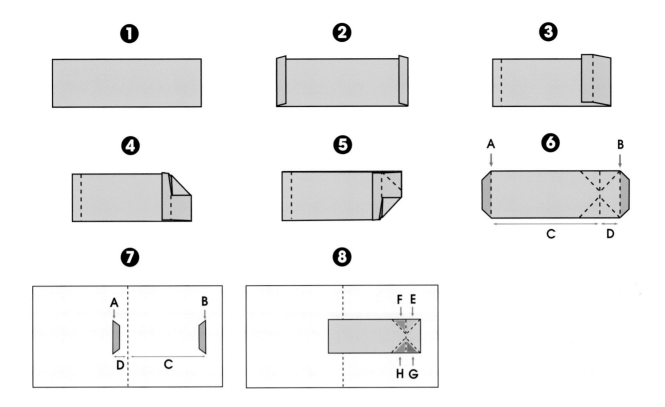

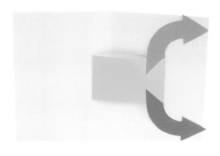

Movement

As the base opens, the movement generated by
each little triangle is different:

- An arm glued to triangle **E** will stay flat against the page
  and rotate in a clockwise direction.

- An arm glued to triangle **G** will stay flat against the page
  and rotate in an anti-clockwise direction.

- Arms glued to triangles **F** and **H** flip over rather than
  rotating against the page.

- As the base closes they all move towards the spine.

18.1 Masking the mechanism

When the arm is glued to **E** or **G** the mechanism that moves the arm
can be hidden by gluing a slightly bigger piece of card onto the long
section of the Parallelogram. This may simply jut out beyond the end
of the Parallelogram, or it can be extended and strengthened by
forming it into another Parallelogram of the same depth.

18.2 Arms glued to the outer gully

This variation uses small double-triangles, folded into the gully formed outside the Parallelogram, where it is attached to the base. To create the gully, the Parallelogram's gluing-tab is made wider and is glued to the base pointing away from the spine.

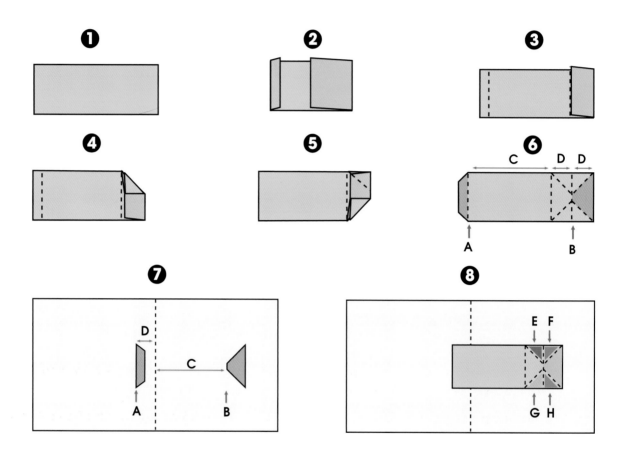

Construction method

This is much the same as the previous mechanism. On this the gluing-tab at one end is the same width as the short side of the Parallelogram. The little triangles that support Moving arms are folded into the gully formed between the short side of the Parallelogram and the extra-sized gluing-tab.

1 Take a piece of card.

2 Fold a gluing-tab onto one end. At the other end fold a vertical crease about 2in (50mm) from the end.

3 Unfold the card, then refold it so that the end is flush with the crease.

4 With the end section still folded, fold over the top corner.

5 Fold over the bottom corner in the same way.

6 Unfold the card.

7 Shows the measurements for positioning the gluing-tabs.

8 With the base flat, glue the piece to the base. The Moving arms glue to any, or all, of the little triangles, **E**, **F**, **G** and **H**.

Movement

- An arm glued to triangle **E** will stay flat against the page and rotate in an anti-clockwise direction.

- An arm glued to triangle **G** will stay flat against the page and rotate in a clockwise direction.

- Arms glued to triangles **F** and **H** flip over rather than rotating against the page.

- As the base closes they all move away from the spine.

- Arms glued to the back of triangles **E** and **G** can be made to fold away behind the Parallelogram as the base opens – the viewer gets a glimpse and then they disappear.

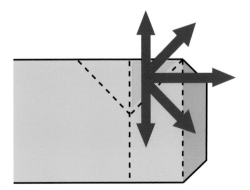

The angle at which the arm, or several arms, juts out from the small triangle it's attached to can also be varied; this in turn will effect the movement.

DESIGN CONSIDERATIONS: HOW THE ARM PROJECTS

The Moving arm is a subtle and tricky mechanism. To fully understand its potential and to be able to incorporate it successfully into your pop-up designs, it is well worth experimenting with it.

18.3 Arms powered by a V-fold and a Counter-fold

Moving arms can also be powered by mechanisms with converging creases. Just as the Parallelogram flattens out when the base is flat, a V-fold with angles that are the same as the angles on the base will flatten out when the base is flat – the same principle applies to Counter-folds.

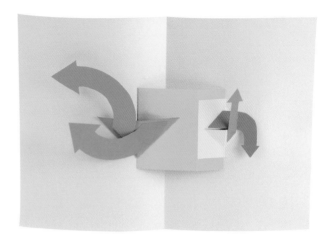

The arms on the left of the picture are powered by a V-fold, those on the right by a Counter-fold.

1 In the example shown here, a V-fold and a Counter-fold have been mounted on gullies formed by a Parallelogram. These gullies, **A** and **A**, on the Parallelogram work in the same way as the spine-fold: when the base is flat, they are flat.

2 Take a piece of card to make a Pointed V-fold.

3 Fold it in half.

4 Fold it again, this time diagonally.

5 Unfold it.

6 Trim it to shape leaving two gluing-tabs. The angles **B** should be approximately 45°.

7 To make the Counter-fold piece see page 112.

8 Both the V-fold and the Counter-fold are glued to the base flat. Angles **B** on the base/Parallelogram are the same as angles **B** on the V-fold. When gluing these in place, make sure that their central folds **C** are aligned with the gullies, **A**.

9 Moving arms can be glued to any of the little triangles, **D**.

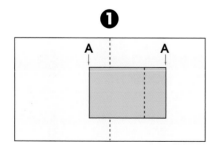

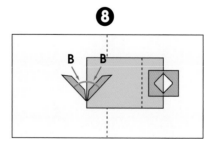

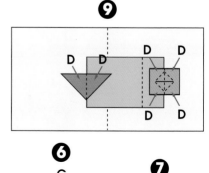

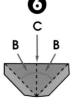
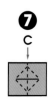

18.4 Arm attached to base

1 The arm is a simple strip with a gluing-tab, **A**, at one end.

2 Glue tab **B** on the parallelogram into place, parallel with the spine. Then glue tab **A** into place – it should be at 45° to the spine.

3 Glue the other end of the Parallelogram into place. If necessary trim the end of the arm so that it can swing down behind the Parallelogram.

Perhaps the most simple of the Moving-arm variations: the arm is glued to the base close to the spine-fold and behind a Parallelogram.

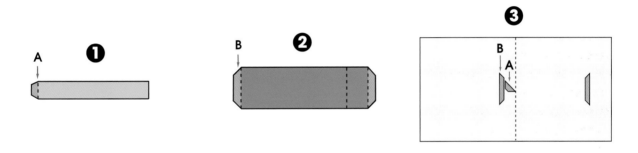

Here Moving arms have been glued on to all four of the little triangles built into the Parallelogram.

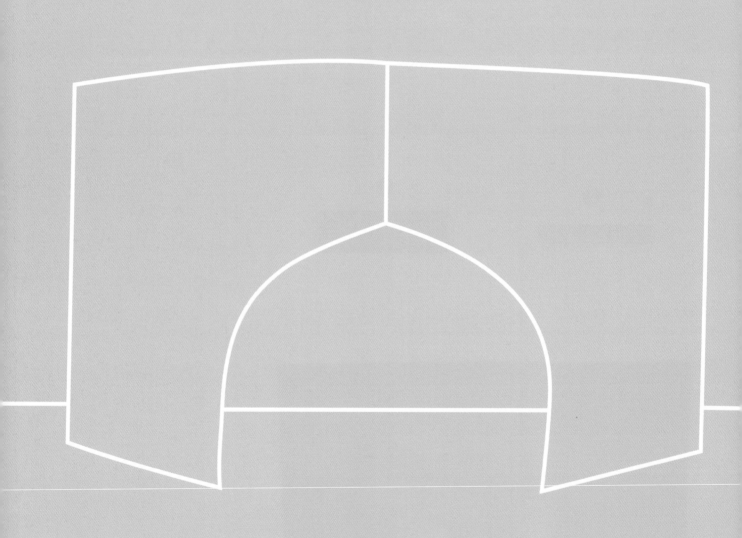

building techniques

The Foundation Shapes are the core of most pop-up designs. Together they form a set of abstract mechanisms that can be used to raise an array of planes, Mountain-folds and gullies in a variety of configurations. This chapter explains the techniques for building with these shapes.

Start by building a Foundation Shape. Visualizing design potential and recognizing difficulties is easiest with a three-dimensional model. To explore the possible ways to modify and extend a shape, go through this checklist:

→ Look at the model from all angles – there is no correct front, back, top or sides. The base may be the ground that the pop-up rises from, or it may form the background.

→ Lengths and angles can be adjusted – modifying them can create very different variations of the same basic shape.

→ Edges can be cut to enhance visual effect – simple, straight, jagged or wild – the only consideration is that edges mustn't snag when the spread is closed.

→ Planes can be extended by sticking on additional pieces – large, small or jutting out.

→ Gullies are the key to pop-up design, since they can have more pop-ups built onto them, which in turn generate more gullies.

→ Mountain-folds can raise folded pieces. They can also be cut into and then folded to generate more small planes, gullies and Mountain-folds.

→ Extra folded pieces can be added, either as part of the visual effect or to introduce additional planes that can then raise larger pieces.

→ Mechanisms can be combined – all the Foundation Shapes are built onto gullies and, since they also create gullies, they can be built onto each other. Highly complex pop-ups are usually constructed by combining several Foundation Shapes.

Building Technique 1

Cutting parts away

The simplest way to modify a pop-up shape is to cut parts away. As most of the Foundation Shapes are remarkably rigid, they can have large 'windows' cut into them.

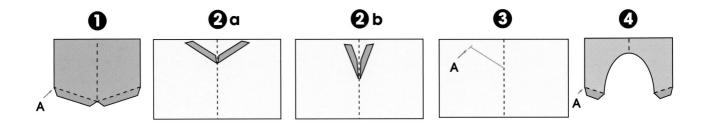

Cutting a V-fold to make an arch

1 Make a V-fold (either Acute-angle, Foundation Shape 2, page 32; or Right-angle, Foundation Shape 1, page 30).

2 Experiment with its position on the page. Do you want a wide shape or a narrow shape?

3 Having decided where the piece is going to go, place its central crease on the spine-fold and mark where one side is going to glue down. It's important to mark the line showing the angle to the spine-fold and especially the end point of the gluing-tab **A**.

4 Cut away the central section of the V-fold.

5 Glue the tab to the page, make sure points **A** are accurately aligned.

6 Follow the usual gluing procedure – fold the pop-up piece into its closed position, put glue on the other tab, then close the base firmly.

1.1 Making part of the pop-up jut out from the central crease

This technique works for any Mountain-fold – in this example it is applied to a V-fold.

1 Draw the pop-up shape: the outline, the central fold line, the sections that will jut out and the gluing-tabs.

2 Score the central fold between the cut lines, apart from where the sections are going to jut out. Rub out the superfluous parts of the guide line.

3 Use a craft-knife to cut round the jutting areas first, then cut out the whole shape.

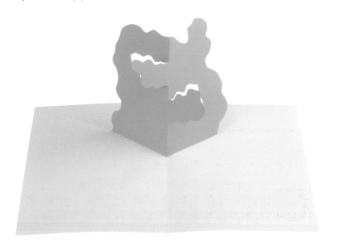

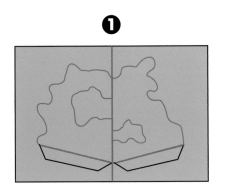

❶

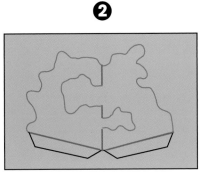

❷

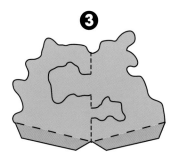

❸

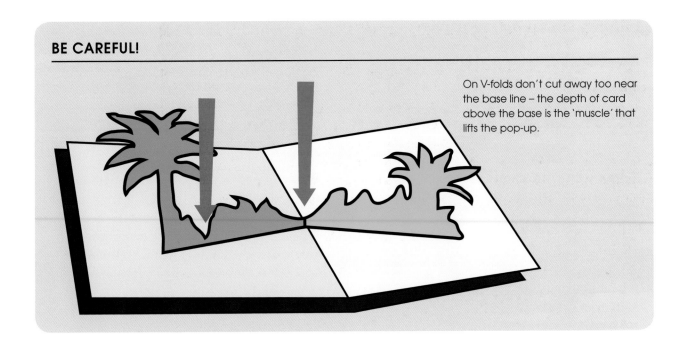

BE CAREFUL!

On V-folds don't cut away too near the base line – the depth of card above the base is the 'muscle' that lifts the pop-up.

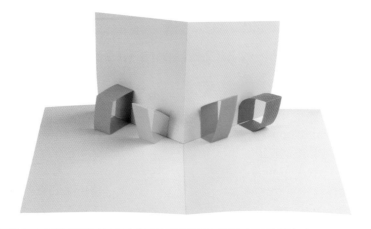

Sticking pieces on

At the most simple level, any pop-up plane can be extended by gluing a flat piece of card onto it. More complex effects can be achieved by gluing small pop-up pieces into the gullies of a pop-up: these pieces may be part of the design, or they may be used as the 'muscles' to raise larger planes at a variety of angles. The small pieces follow the basic pop-up principles, based on either Parallel-folds or V-folds. All the examples shown here start with a small piece of card folded in half.

Adding small Parallel-fold pieces

These all start with a strip of card. Although any size will do, a good starting point would be approximately 3in (76mm) long by ½in (13mm) wide. These first two steps are the same for the four variations.

❶ **❷** **❸** **❹**

Square-shaped addition

1 Take a strip of card.

2 Fold it in half.

3 Fold it in half again.

4 When opened out the two end sections are the gluing-tabs.

5 When gluing this into place make sure that the ends of the piece are flush with the gully. This ensures that the lengths are balanced on each side of the gully.

2.1 Kite-shaped addition

1 Take a strip of card.

2 Fold it in half.

3 Fold it again but make the new crease nearer to the strip's ends, not in the middle.

4 When opened out the two end sections, the gluing-tabs, are shorter than the two middle sections. This produces a kite shape.

5 The gluing method is the same as page 98.

2.2 Asymmetric addition

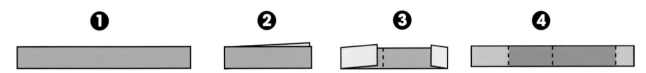

1 Take a strip of card.

2 Fold it in half.

3 Unfold it – then fold each end in separately, but not equally.

4 When unfolded the strip has four different lengths.

5 The gluing method is the same as page 98.

2.3 Curved addition

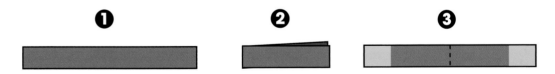

1 Take a strip of card.

2 Fold it in half.

3 This variation only has one fold, in the centre. Put glue on the two ends and ensure that they are flush with the gully.

4 If desired, this shape can be made asymmetric by putting more glue on one side than the other.

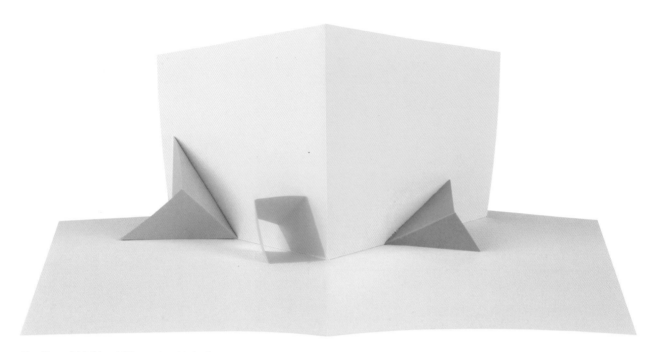

The three V-fold additions glued into the gully formed where an Acute-angle V-fold is attached to the page.

Adding small V-fold pieces

To make angle-fold pieces, initially try using rectangular pieces approximately 4in (100mm) long and 2in (51mm) wide.

2.4 Regular V-fold addition

1 Take a rectangle of card.

2 Fold it in half.

3 Fold it diagonally, corner to corner.

4 When they are opened out, the two outer triangles are the gluing-tabs.

5 When gluing, make sure side **A – A** is flush against the gully.

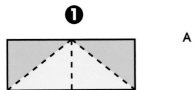

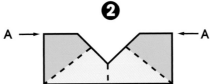

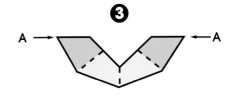

2.5 Removing the point of the V-fold addition

1 Start with a piece like step 4 (facing page).

2 Cut away around the point where all the fold lines meet. Make sure that some of line **A** is left intact on each side.

3 The outer sections are the gluing-tabs. The piece may be trimmed to shape but make sure that sides **A** and **A** remain.

4 When gluing, make sure sides **A** and **A** are flush against the gully.

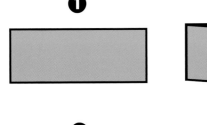

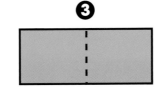

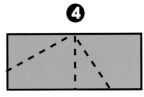

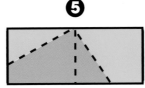

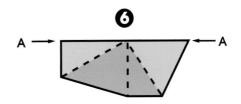

2.6 Asymmetric V-fold addition

1 Take a rectangle of card.

2 Fold it in half.

3 Unfold it.

4 Fold two more angled creases, at different angles to the central fold, but meeting the central fold at the edge of the card.

5 The outer triangles are the gluing-tabs.

6 Trim the piece to shape. Leave line **A** – **A** intact, as this is the edge that glues flush into the gully.

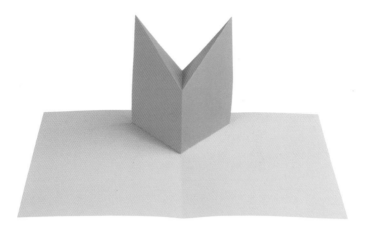

Building Technique 3

Extra creases

Angled creases can be built into a pop-up, either to modify the basic shape, or else to create extra planes and gullies for building on.

Symmetrical angled creases

❶   **❷**   **❸**   **❹**   **❺**   **❻**   **❼**

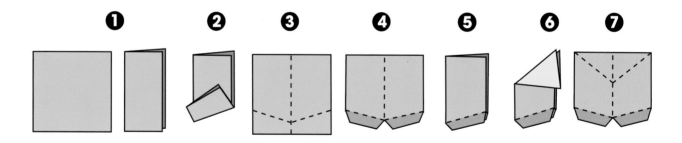

1–4 These steps are used to make a simple Acute-angle V-fold (Foundation Shape 2, page 32, 1, 2, 3 and 4).

5 Fold the pop-up in half.

6 Fold the top corner over, and crimp, to create symmetrical angled creases.

7 Unfold the card.

8 Re-fold the card so that the central fold is half Valley-fold and half Mountain-fold.

9 Experiment with the shape on the page. Glue one side, fold the piece into its closed position, glue the other side, close the base and press firmly.

Adjusting the Angled creases

Changing the angle of these extra creases will produce different gullies above the page.

3.1 Top as a gully pointing down

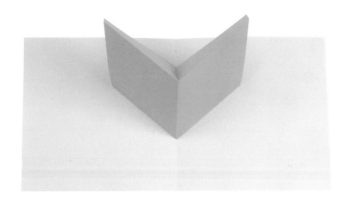

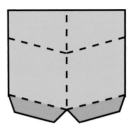

If the new creases are parallel with the creases on the gluing-tabs, the new gully will angle back downwards towards the base.

3.2 Top as a Mountain-fold

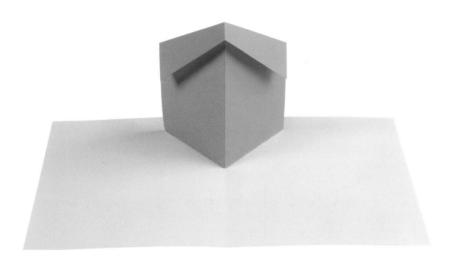

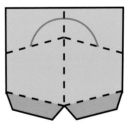

When the angles above the two new creases add up to more than 180°, the top folds forwards as a Mountain-fold.

3.3 Extra creases on a Parallel-fold

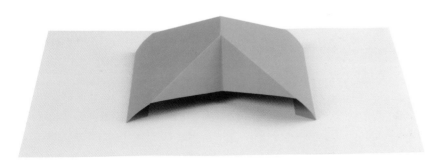

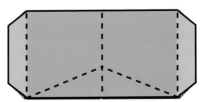

The same technique can be applied to Parallel-folds.

3.4 Adding asymmetric angled creases

Because these are asymmetric the building process can't start by simply folding a piece of card in half. These have to start with drawing.

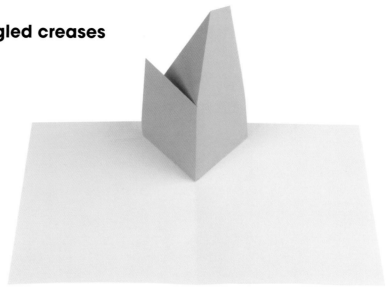

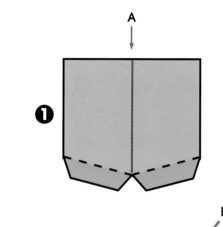

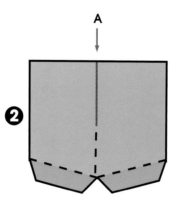

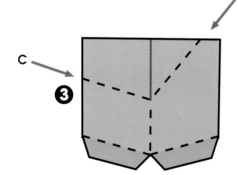

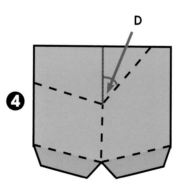

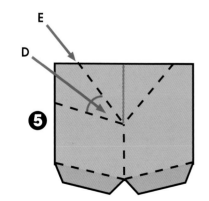

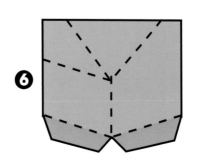

1 Draw – but don't score – the central fold line **A** of the pop-up piece (an Acute-angle V-fold, Foundation Shape 2).

2 Score line **A** from the bottom of the piece to about half way up.

3 Score two more lines – **B** and **C** – at different angles to the central crease.

4 Measure the angle **D** between lines **A** and **B**.

5 Measure the angle **D** above line **C**. Draw and score line **E** above line **C**.

6 Erase the top of line **A**, where it has not been scored.

7 Fold and crimp all the creases – **A**, **B** and **C** are all Mountain-folds, **E** is a Valley-fold.

8 Glue the piece to the base using the method shown on page 17.

3.5 Using angled creases to make gluing-tabs

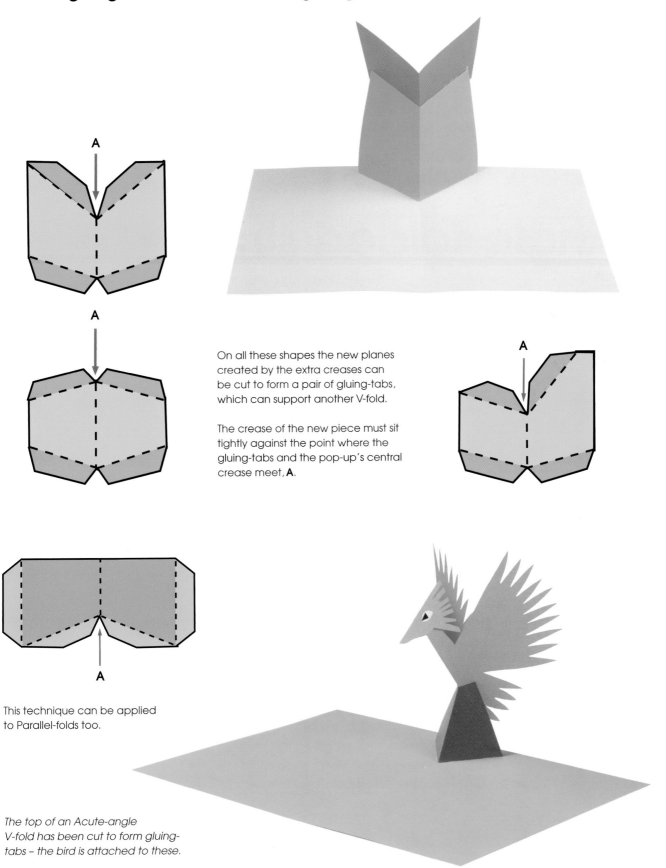

On all these shapes the new planes created by the extra creases can be cut to form a pair of gluing-tabs, which can support another V-fold.

The crease of the new piece must sit tightly against the point where the gluing-tabs and the pop-up's central crease meet, **A**.

This technique can be applied to Parallel-folds too.

The top of an Acute-angle V-fold has been cut to form gluing-tabs – the bird is attached to these.

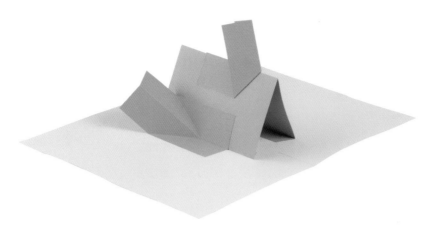

Building Technique 4

Angle-folded strips

These small versatile pieces have a lot of sculptural potential. They can either be used to add three-dimensional detail to a larger pop-up, or as extensions for supporting larger additions.

1 Initially try using strips about 2in (51mm) wide and 4in (100mm) long.

2 Fold the piece of card in half lengthways.

3 Fold an angle into the piece, then crimp it thoroughly.

4 Flatten the piece out.

5 Re-fold so that the central fold is half Valley-fold and half Mountain-fold.

❶

❷

❸

❹

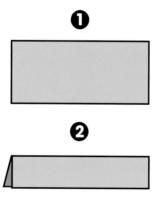

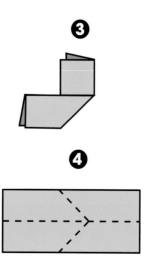

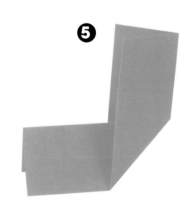

The strip is folded into the shape of an L. One arm has a Mountain-fold on the inside and a Valley-fold on the outside, the other arm has a Valley-fold on the inside and a Mountain-fold on the outside. This makes it possible to glue them into or onto almost any pop-up fold.

4.1 Acute fold

The shapes of these pieces can be adjusted by making the fold at step 3 (see facing page) more acute or more obtuse.

4.2 Obtuse fold

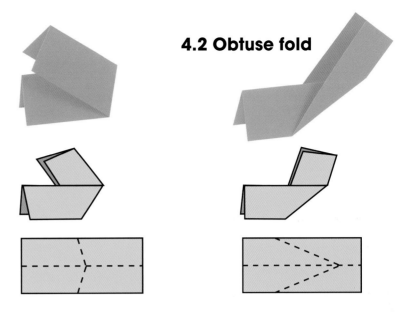

Add more creases

After step 3, the piece can be folded again. There are three possible variations of these creases. They can all be modified by changing the size and shape of the card and, most importantly, by adjusting the angles of the creases.

A LIMITATION!

The more folds there are between the spine-fold and the extensions, the less the gullies at the extremities will open. This is due to the bendiness of the card: thorough scoring and creasing helps alleviate the problem.

4.3 Creases point the same way

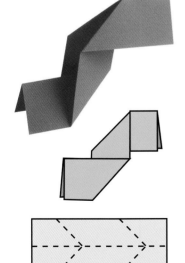

4.4 Creases point apart

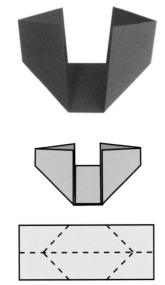

4.5 Creases point together

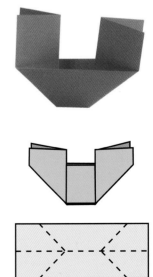

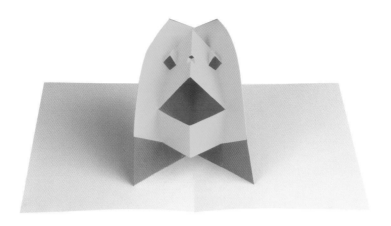

Building Technique 5

Counter-folds

A Counter-fold is a pop-up made from one piece of card. It can be made as a small additional piece that is glued into a gully on a pop-up, or it can be built into a design by adding extra cuts and creases to the folds of a pop-up before it is glued into place. On Counter-folds it is always the position and angle of the creases that is important; the cuts can be any shape.

Symmetrical Counter-folds

The method for making all the Symmetrical Counter-folds is the same.

1 Take a piece of card – try using half or quarter of an A4 sheet, or even smaller.

2 Fold the card in half and crease it well.

3 Make the cut, or cuts, into the folded edge of the piece of card. Experiment with the shape and angle of these.

4 Fold the section of card back as shown in the diagrams. Crease it very thoroughly.

5 Open out the card.

6 Re-fold the card with the pop-up section pushed forward.

5.1 One cut with angled creases

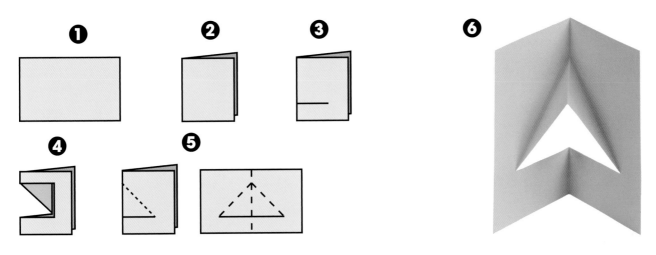

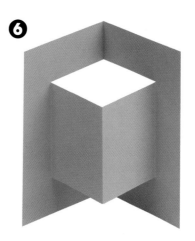

5.2 One short cut and one long cut with angled creases

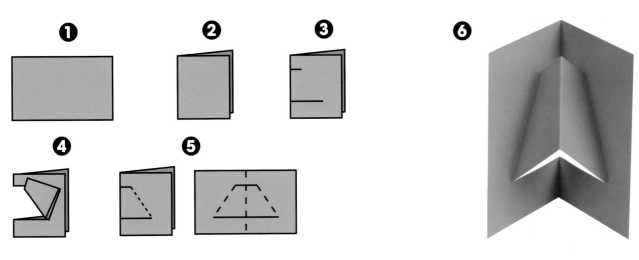

5.3 Two cuts with parallel creases

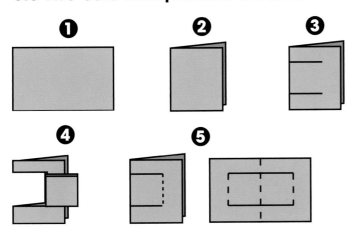

Asymmetric Counter-folds

These Asymmetric Counter-folds have to be measured, drawn and scored, since the central fold of the base does not continue across the pop-up section.

①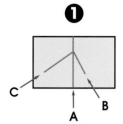
C
A B

②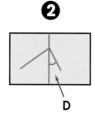
D

③④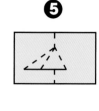
E
F

⑤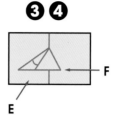

5.4 Asymmetric angled creases

1 Draw the central fold line **A** and the asymmetric lines of the creases **B** and **C**.

2 Measure the angle **D** between lines **A** and **B**.

3 Measure the same angle from **C** and draw in the fold line **E**.

4 Draw the cut line **F** and erase the central fold line where it crosses the pop-up section.

5 Score and cut along the lines marked.

6 Fold the base and push the pop-up piece forward.

①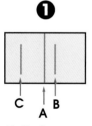
C B
A

②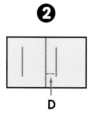
D

③④
F
F
E

⑤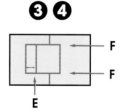

5.5 Asymmetric parallel creases

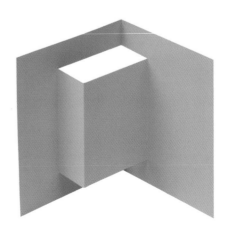

1 Draw the central fold line **A** and the lines of the creases **B** and **C** – these are parallel to **A**, but at different distances from it.

2 Measure the length **D** between lines **A** and **B**.

3 Measure the same distance from **C**. Draw in fold line **E**.

4 Draw the cut lines **F** and erase the central fold line where it crosses the pop-up section.

5 Score and cut along the lines marked.

6 Fold the base and push the pop-up piece forward.

Using Counter-folded pieces

Counter-folded pieces are very useful when designing pop-ups, as:

- They are quick and easy to make.

- Pre-planning isn't necessary for the symmetrical ones.

- They can be glued into any gully on a pre-existing pop-up.

- They may be big, bold and part of the design – even bigger than the Foundation Shape that is used to raise them.

- Or they may be small and discreet, used as the muscle to lift other large pieces.

- Experiment with Counter-folds when considering what additional planes or gullies to add to a Foundation Shape.

- When additional angled planes are needed for a design, the effects produced by a variety of angles can be simply tested by using Counter-folds.

When gluing these versatile pieces into place, it is important to make sure that the spine-fold of the Counter-folded piece is flush with the gully it is being glued into.

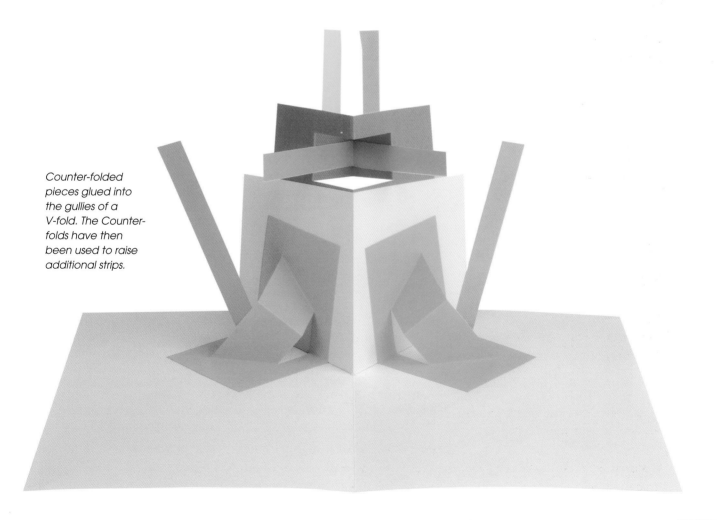

Counter-folded pieces glued into the gullies of a V-fold. The Counter-folds have then been used to raise additional strips.

Multiple Counter-folds

Some pop-up designs are composed entirely of multiple Counter-folds.

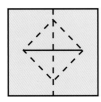

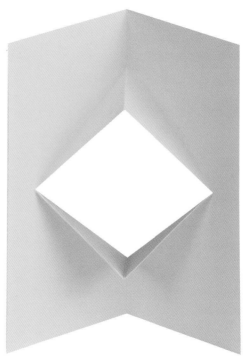

5.6 One cut and double angle creases

A simple variant of 5.1, with two Counter-folds working off one cut to produce an elementary mouth effect.

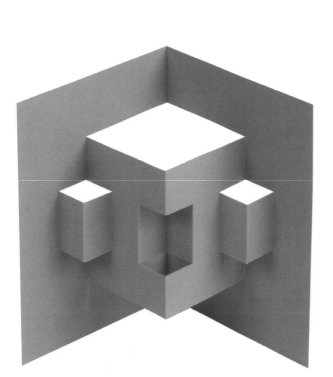

  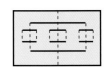

5.7 Simple multiple parallel Counter-folds

Just as pop-ups create gullies that other pop-ups can be glued into, Counter-folds produce gullies that more Counter-folds can be cut into. To make this one, start with a simple 5.3 and then add smaller cuts to its fold lines.

5.8 A version of 5.2 – in this case mounted on an Obtuse-angle V-fold

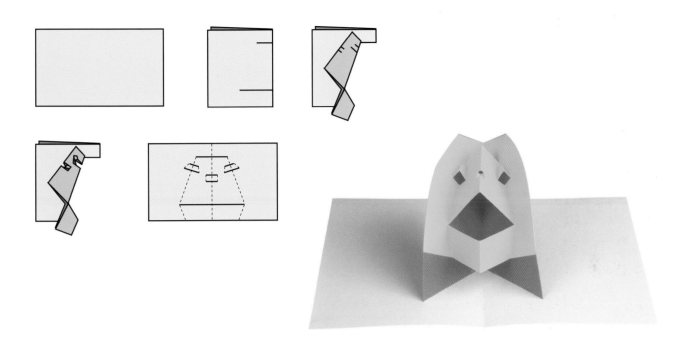

5.9 Pre-planned Counter-folds cut into the folds of a bigger pop-up

Simple Counter-folds have been added to both the central crease of this V-fold and the gluing-tabs that attach it to the page.

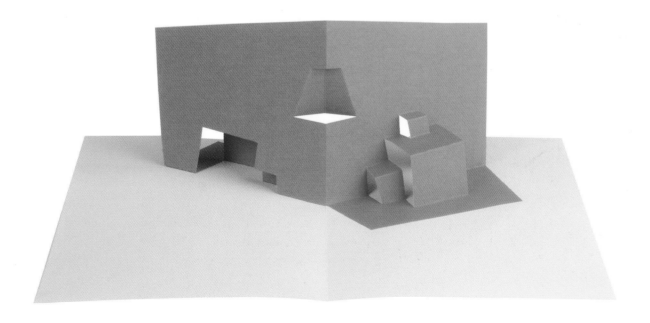

5.10 Counter-folding multiple Parallelograms

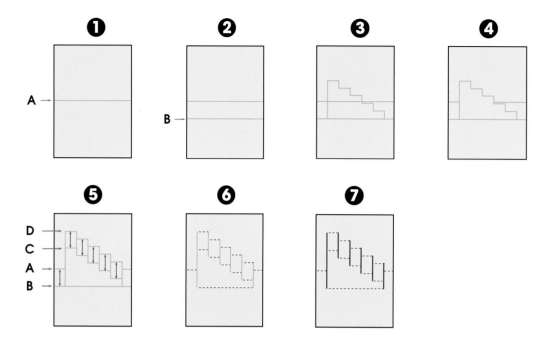

1 Draw, but don't score, the central fold line, **A**.

2 Below it draw the bottom line, **B**, of the pop-up section.

3 Draw the front elevation of the pop-up.

4 Rub out the section of the central fold line that lies within the pop-up.

5 Measure the distance between line **A** and **B**. Then measure the same distance above the line of the top step **C** and draw line **D**. Repeat for each step of the pop-up.

6 Score the fold lines. They must never cross cut lines.

7 Make the cuts. The cut lines must end at fold lines.

8 Push the piece into shape.

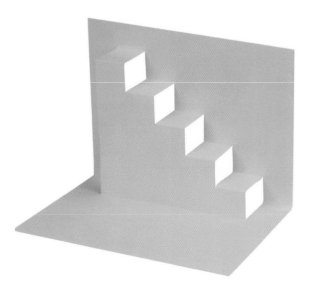

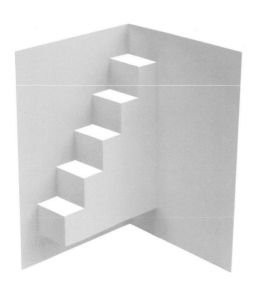

5.11 Multiple Parallelograms with jutting additions

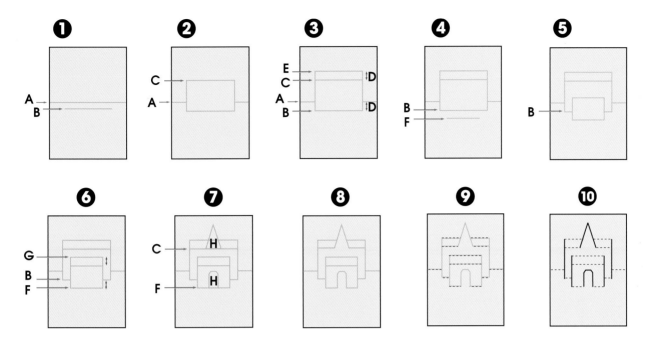

1 Draw the central fold line, **A**. Below it draw the bottom of the first pop-up step, **B**.

2 Draw the front elevation of the first step, and erase the central fold line within it. The top line of the front elevation is **C**.

3 Measure the distance, **D**, between the central crease and the bottom line of the pop-up. Draw another line, **E**, the same distance above line **C**.

4 Below line **B** draw the bottom line, **F**, of the second pop-up step.

5 Draw the front elevation of the second step. Erase the section of line **B** within this box.

6 Measure the distance between lines **B** and **F** and draw line **G** the same distance above this second step.

7 Add the jutting extensions, **H**. The one added to line **C** will jut up from the pop-up, the one added to line **F** will jut into the pop up.

8 Erase lines **C** and **F** at the base of the jutting sections.

9 Score the fold lines. They must never cross cut lines.

10 Make the cuts. The cut lines must end at fold lines.

11 Push the pop-up sections forward and fold the card down to establish the folds.

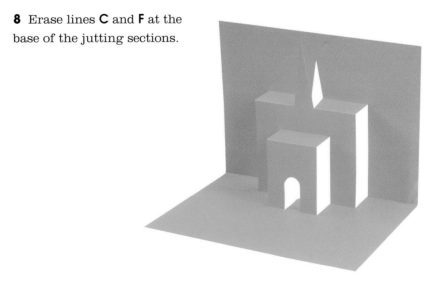

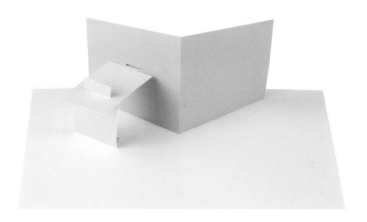

Building Technique 6

Slots

A slot is used when one piece of card juts out through another piece and needs to be able to move freely. When both pieces of card lie flat, as in pull-strip mechanisms, then a simple slit is fine.

THE SLOT

A slot is usually ¹/₁₆–¹/₈ in (1–2mm) wide, enough to accommodate the thickness of the piece of card jutting through it and allow the piece to move easily. A simple slit will cause the plane to grip the piece jutting through it.

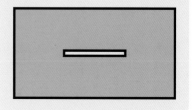

6.1 Jutting through a Parallel-fold

1 Take a strip of card and fold a gluing-tab onto one end of it, **A**.

2 Make a Parallel-fold piece (Foundation Shape 6, page 42). Cut a slot, **B**, in this piece. The slot should be parallel with the creases and wide enough to let the strip slide through it easily.

3 Glue the strip to the base, **C**. Thread the strip through the slot and glue the Parallel-fold to the page. (For gluing, see page 17.)

4 The point at which it is glued, **C**, must be parallel to the spine. In this example it is flush with the spine. It can, however, be placed anywhere between the other two gluing-strips – its position dictates the angle that the strip juts out at.

5 As the page closes, the Parallel-fold rises up away from the spine, while the jutting piece slides down through the slot.

Pop-up Design and Paper Mechanics

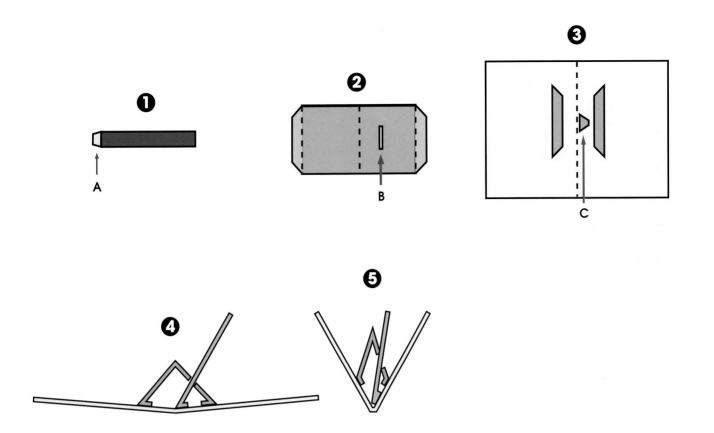

As long as it remains parallel to the spine, the strip can be glued to the base at any point under the Parallel-fold. Every position will make it jut out at a different angle.

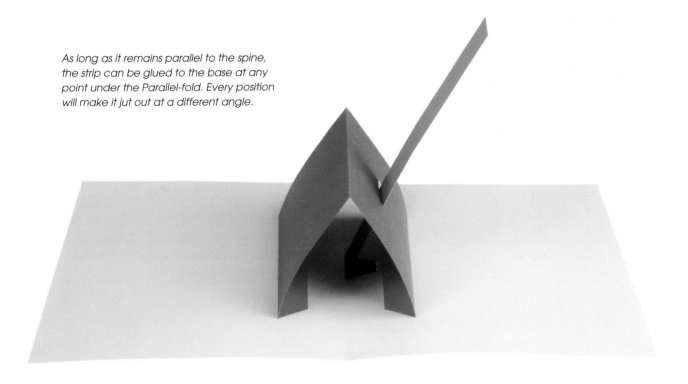

6.2 Jutting through a Mountain-fold

The key to this mechanism is a little piece with two arms. It is folded down the middle and the arms jut through a pair of small slots on each side of the Mountain-fold.

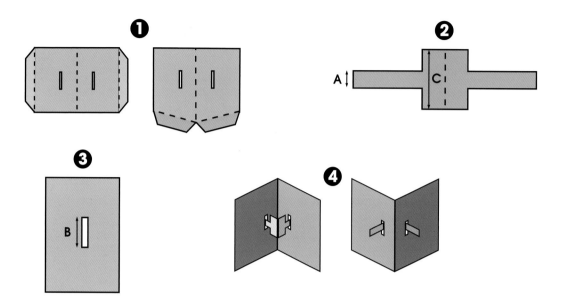

1 Start by making the main body of the pop-up. These two examples are made with a Parallel-fold (Foundation Shape 6, page 42) and a V-fold piece (Foundation Shape 2, page 32). The mechanism will work with any Mountain-fold.

2 Make the small jutting piece with its two arms.

3 Cut the two slots, **B**, on each side of the Mountain-fold. Make sure length **A** is smaller than **B**, so the arms can move freely, and that length **C** is longer than **B**, so the jutting piece can't drift through the slots.

4 Push the arms through the slots from behind the Mountain-fold.

5 Glue larger pieces of card to the ends of the arms to stop them slipping back through the slots.

6 Glue the pop-up to the page, using the sticking method explained with the relevant Foundation Shape (see page 17).

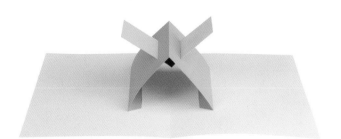

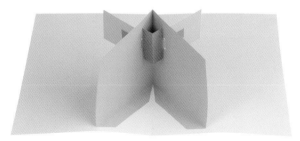

6.3 Jutting through a V-fold horizontally

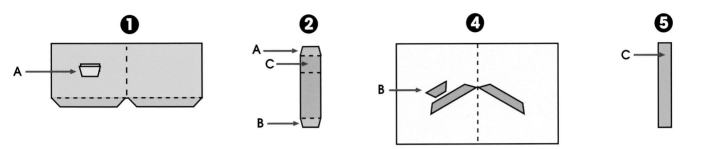

1 Make a V-fold piece, in this example Foundation Shape 1 (page 30).

2 Make a Parallelogram piece to glue behind the V-fold (see Foundation Shape 7.2, page 49).

3 At the point, **A**, where the Parallelogram will glue onto the V-fold, cut a horizontal slot.

4 Glue the V-fold to the base and the Parallelogram into place.

5 Push the projecting piece through the slot and glue the end section, **C**, to the top of the Parallelogram.

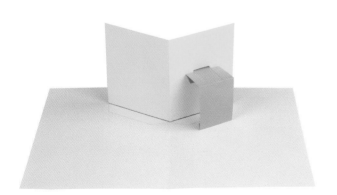

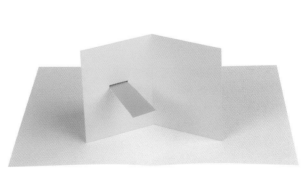

6.4 Horizontal piece on the side of a V-fold

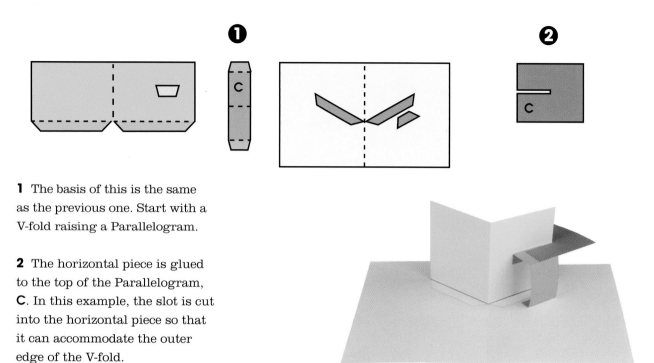

1 The basis of this is the same as the previous one. Start with a V-fold raising a Parallelogram.

2 The horizontal piece is glued to the top of the Parallelogram, **C**. In this example, the slot is cut into the horizontal piece so that it can accommodate the outer edge of the V-fold.

6.5 Interlocked pieces projecting from a Mountain-fold

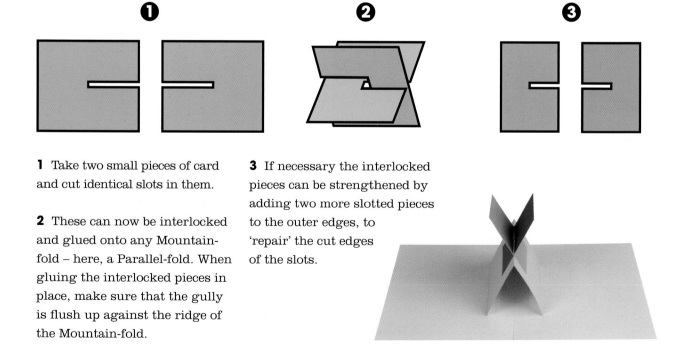

1 Take two small pieces of card and cut identical slots in them.

2 These can now be interlocked and glued onto any Mountain-fold – here, a Parallel-fold. When gluing the interlocked pieces in place, make sure that the gully is flush up against the ridge of the Mountain-fold.

3 If necessary the interlocked pieces can be strengthened by adding two more slotted pieces to the outer edges, to 'repair' the cut edges of the slots.

6.6 Wing-tab joint

This kind of joint is strong and moves more freely than a creased gluing-tab. If the point to be joined is small, or there are numerous joints on a design, this will often be the type of joint to use.

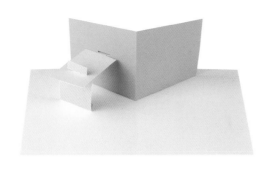

❶

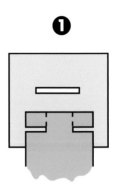

❷

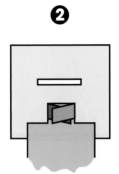

❸

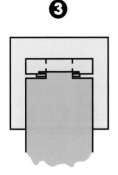

1 Instead of a gluing-tab the piece being attached has two little flaps on the end. The piece it's being attached to has a short slot.

2 The little flaps are folded over (not creased) and pushed through the slot.

3 The two little flaps are then unfolded behind the slot.

6.7 Wing-tab variation

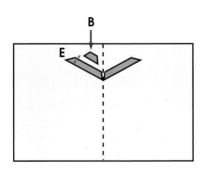

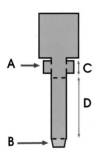

For this alternative way of constructing 6.3 (Jutting through a V-fold horizontally) the V-fold has a slot in it parallel with the base. The jutting projection and the Parallelogram behind the V-fold are made of one piece of card. Next to the projecting section are two little wing-tabs,

A, these are separated from the projection by two slots approximately 1/16in (2mm) wide. The rest of the piece, **C** and **D**, form the Parallelogram. The only gluing-tab, **B**, is on the end.

To construct: fold the wing-tabs over; push the Parallelogram

section through the slot in the V-fold; unfold the wing-tabs and glue **B** to the base.

To make the jutting piece horizontal, ensure that **C** = **E** and **D** = **F**. To raise it at an angle, follow the asymmetric principle (see pages 50–51): **E** + **D** = **C** + **F**.

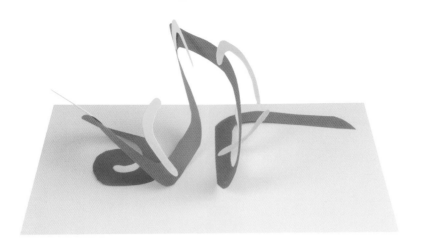

Bending planes

By far the most common form of Bending plane is the Spiral, probably the easiest pop-up to make. It has no creases and is excellent for creating a wild and energetic effect. They can't be used as the muscle to lift other mechanisms; however, small flat pieces can be stuck onto them.

7.1 Spirals

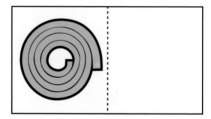 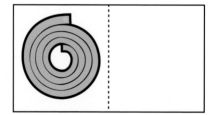 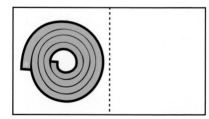

1 Cut out the Spiral; whether long or short, it must be narrow enough to be able to twist.

2 Position it on the page. Where the ends of the piece lie in relation to the spine-fold (see diagrams above) determines the shape that the spiral will make when the page opens. It's worth experimenting, as the results can be dramatically different.

3 Put glue on the underside of one end of the piece and stick it to the base.

4 Put glue on the top of the other end. Close and press firmly.

OTHER POSSIBILITIES

Spirals can be stuck onto other pop-ups, between any two planes that move apart as the base opens. The sticking method is always the same.

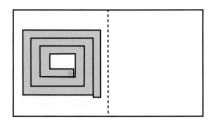

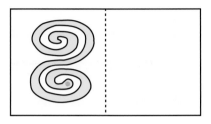

The piece is usually made as a spiral – however, as shown above, it can be more or less any shape, so long as the piece of card is long, narrow and bendy.

Several pieces can be used in an elegant tangle on one spread.

7.2 Working with the flattening gully

Most pop-ups are glued into gullies that close as the base closes – this one is the opposite. It has to be built onto the type of gully that opens out flat as the base closes.

❶

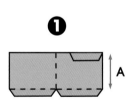

A

❷

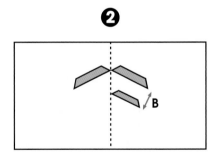

B

❸

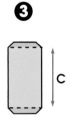

C

1 Make and measure the height, **A**, of a Right-angle V-fold.

2 The distance on the base between the V-fold and the Bending plane's gluing position = **B**.

3 The length of the Bending plane **C** = **A** + **B**.

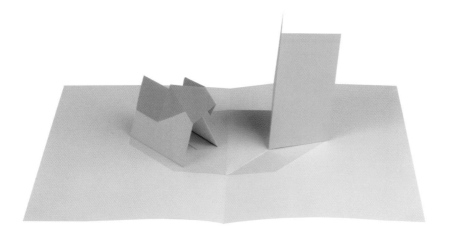

Building Technique 8

Straps

The spine-fold gully lies flat when the base is opened out flat. Straps are used to create similar gullies off-centre, making it possible to build pop-up structures onto the base in different positions, rather than always spanning the spine. The idea is very simple – if the angles on a V-fold piece, or the lengths on a Parallel-fold piece are the same as those on the base, the piece will lie flat when the base is open.

 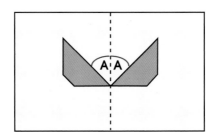 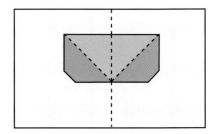

8.1 Symmetrical V-fold Strap

All four angles, **A**, are the same. The gluing-tabs are broad; they lie flat on the page, not folded underneath, which gives a smoother gully to glue pop-ups onto.

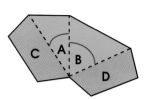

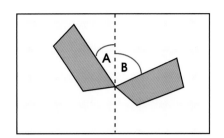

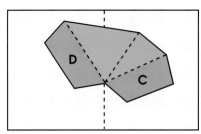

8.2 Asymmetric V-fold Strap

Angles **A** on the pop-up piece and on the base are the same. Angles **B** on the base and the pop-up piece are the same. With the piece flat, the big angle on the piece glues down over the small angle on the page and the small angle on the piece glues down over the big angle on the page.

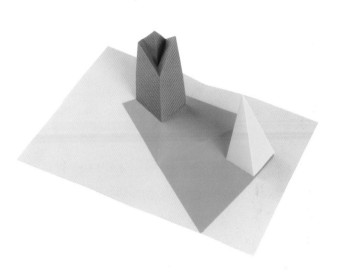

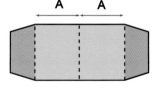

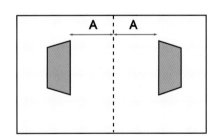

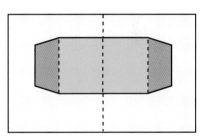

8.3 Parallel-fold Strap

Lengths **A** on the strap and the base are all the same. The asymmetric variant of the Parallel-fold Strap is the Parallelogram.

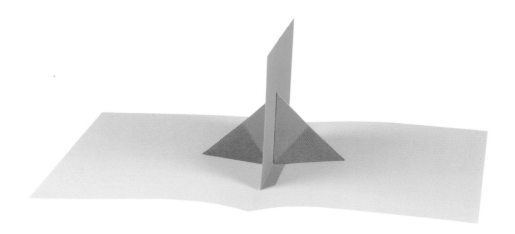

45-degree folds

The 45-degree fold is a variation of the V-fold that is used to fill or span a 'corner' (see illustrations). Two of these pieces can be used in opposition to raise a plane vertically over a gully.

Raise a plane vertically on the spine

A pair of triangular pieces, each folded to form pairs of 45-degree folds, work in opposition to hold a plane vertically on the spine.

❶ **❷** **❸** **❹a** **❹b** **❺** **❻** **❼**

Making the pieces

1 Take a piece of card and fold a ½in (13mm) strip along the bottom edge to form a gluing-tab.

2 Trim the gluing-tab. This is the vertical plane.

3 Cut a piece of card to make a small right angle triangle.

4 Fold a gluing-tab onto each of the short sides.

5 Fold the piece in half, dividing the right angle into two 45-degree folds.

6 Unfold the triangle.

7 Trim the gluing-tabs on the sides to shape.

8 Make another identical triangular piece.

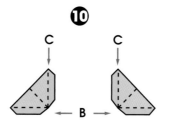

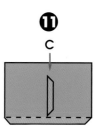

Gluing the pieces on

9 Glue the vertical plane to the base, flush with the spine **A**.

10 Glue the triangular pieces to the base; one on each side, tight against the central plane but at right angles to it, **B** and **B**.

11 Glue the triangles to the central plane, **C** and **C**.

9.1 Vertical plane raising another vertical plane

Here a pre-existing vertical plane (the side of a box) is used to raise another plane at right angles to it.

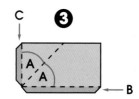

1 Take a piece of card and fold a gluing-tab onto each side of it.

2 Make a diagonal fold that brings the two crease lines together, thus creating two equal angles, **A** and **A**.

3 Place the corner of the piece in the gully and glue **B** to the base and **C** to the upright plane.

Here a double 45-degree fold enables a plane to be raised at right angles to a Box.

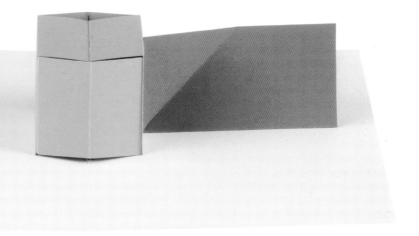

9.2 'Filling' the end of a Parallelogram

The end of a Parallelogram structure can be 'filled in' using a piece of card with a double 45-degree fold.

1 Take a piece of card with a fold, **A**, equally dividing the angle between two gluing-tabs, **C** and **D**. It is important that crease **A** equally divides the angle so that **B** and **B** are both 45 degrees. Crease **A** does not go corner to corner.

2 When the Parallelogram is upright, all four of its corners look the same.

3 As the Parallelogram folds flat two of the corners, type **E**, will fold closed, the other two, type **F**, will flatten out. Make sure that the two gluing-tabs **C** and **D** straddle the **E** type of gully.

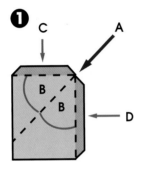

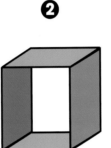

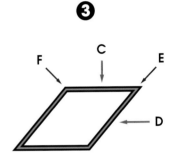

Multiple examples of the 45-degree fold. Here a Parallelogram is constructed with one of its sides rising directly from the spine gully. The Parallelogram is supported by two opposing 45-degree folds, one on each side; another 45-degree fold is deployed to 'fill in' the end of the Parallelogram.

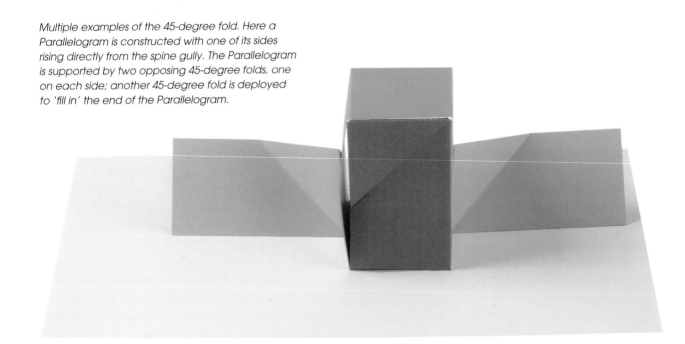

9.3 Box top

This type of Box is derived from the Open-topped shape – the double 45-degree fold is used to give it a flat lid. A Parallelogram below the lid pushes it into shape. The easiest way to construct this is with a ruler and set square.

1 Draw four identical rectangles with fold lines between them. Add gluing-tabs to the bottom edge of two adjacent ones, **C** and **C**, and a gluing-tab on the end, **D**.

2 Make a support pillar, the same height, **B**, as the rectangles. Put a gluing-tab on each end, **E1** and **E2**. Make it double thickness – **F** glues to **F**.

3 Draw a square on top of one of the rectangles, add a gluing-tab, **G**, and a diagonal fold line creating the double 45-degree folds **H** and **H**.

4 Glue **G** first: glue **E1**, parallel to the top of the rectangle, touching and at 45 degrees to the lid's diagonal fold, then glue **D** to **D**.

5 Next, glue the box to the page, starting with **C1** at 45 degrees to the spine. With the whole piece laying flat against the base, **E2** should find its correct position and length **J** should not need to be measured. Now glue **E2** and finally, put glue on **C2**, close the base and press firmly.

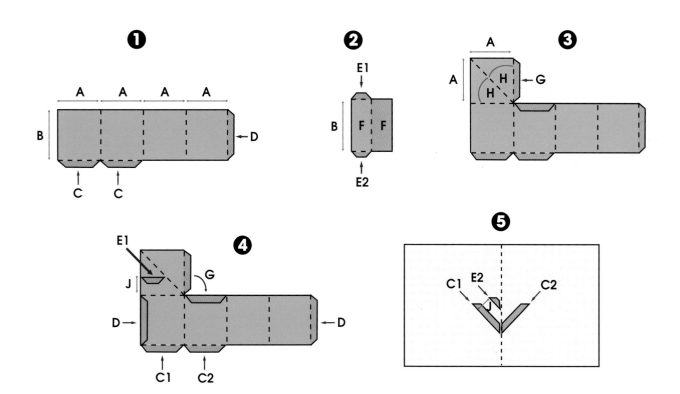

pull-tab mechanisms

These are the mechanisms that slide, turn and flip. They are all activated by pulling a tab – excellent for adding an element of interactivity to a spread.

→ Although normally built onto a flat page, they can also be built onto the plane of a pop-up.

→ They can be used to reveal, or change images.

→ They can make images rock, leap or glide across a page.

→ They can raise three-dimensional pop-ups anywhere on the page.

→ Good for adding extra surprise to a spread.

These mechanisms form a different category from the sculptural Foundation Shapes. To make them, a craft-knife and ruler are essential. They also require more calculation and precision.

Pull-strips

Pull-strips power the two-dimensional mechanisms. Most of the strip lies under the page, with just a small tab showing – pulling the tab activates the mechanism.

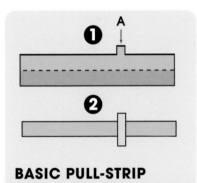

BASIC PULL-STRIP

1 Pull-strips should be made double thickness, and glued, to prevent them buckling when pushed. Most of them have a tab, **A**, jutting out to control how far they can move.

2 Tabs can be made from a small strip of card glued across the Pull-strip.

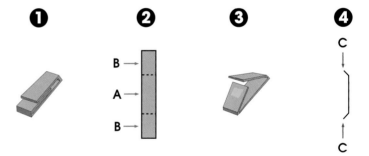

Sleeves and slits

These control the direction of a Pull-strip's movement. Their positioning is important – the tab on the Pull-strip coming up against them controls how far the strip can move.

1 Sleeves and slits should be approximately ¹/₈in (3mm) wider than the Pull-strip – enough to allow it to move freely, but not so much that it can start to 'drift'.

2 Glue the central section, **A**, of the sleeve to the page.

3 The arms, **B**, overlap each other – use a small dab of glue to keep them in place.

4 The slit has a short (about ¹/₈in/3mm) bend at each end – this allows the card to lift slightly to accommodate the Pull-strip.

1.1 Simple changing image

The two images are on the strip – one at a time is seen through a window cut in the page. Pulling the strip changes the image.

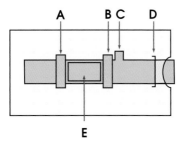

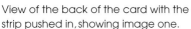

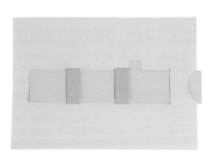

View of the back of the card with the strip pushed in, showing image one.

Position with the strip pulled out showing image two.

A and **B**: The sleeves controlling the direction of the Pull-strip's movement. **C**: The tab controlling the amount of movement. Stopped by **B** when pushed, and **D** when pulled. **D**: The slit.
E: The window in the page.

1.2 Slot-guided slide

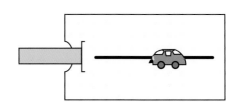

This mechanism is used to make a piece of card glide across the page. It's an unusual Pull-strip mechanism, as it doesn't need sleeves – the configuration of the card ❸ and image hold the strip to the back of the page. The slot in the page governs the amount of movement.

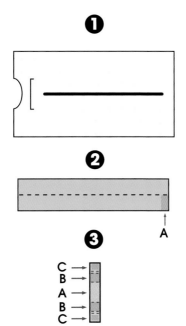

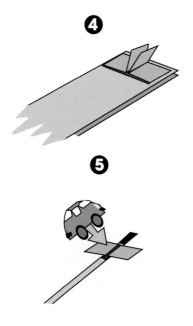

1 The page has a long slot in it (1/16–1/8/2–3mm wide).

2 The Pull-strip is double thickness.

3 A small piece of card glues on to the Pull-strip at **A**.

4 On the small piece of card **B** and **B** fold over and glue on top of **A**. **C** and **C** remain jutting up.

5 **C** and **C** go up through the slot in the base, then fold down flat. The moving image is glued to the top of **C** and **C**.

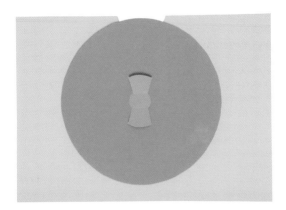

Pivots

The two most useful types of Pivot are the Hub and the Sliding Pivot. The Hub is used to hold pieces of card together while allowing them to rotate. The Sliding Pivot is most often built onto a Pull-strip.

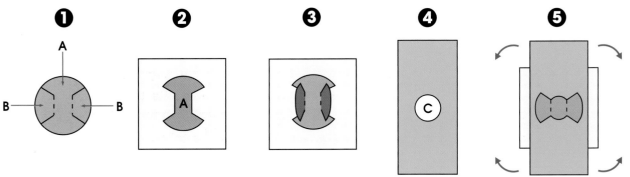

Hub

The Hub is the most commonly used Pivot. Wheels which turn behind a page and most of the two-dimensional articulated designs use Hubs to join the moving pieces.

1 The Hub is a small disc, cut so that it has two arms, **B**, which can fold up and then be flattened out again. The total diameter is about 1in (25mm) and the distance between the creases slightly less than

$\frac{1}{2}$in (13mm). Commercially produced ones are smaller.

2 Glue the main body of the disc, **A**, to the base card.

3 Fold the two arms up.

4 The hole, **C**, in the other piece of card is slightly more than $\frac{1}{2}$in (13mm). The size of this hole is important – if it is too big things will drift, too small and it will grip the

Hub and hinder its movement. Make sure that the edges of the hole are cut very smoothly – a rough or jagged edge can inhibit movement.

5 Pass the arms through the hole in the card – then fold them out flat again.

If necessary a small additional piece of card can be glued flat on top of the arms, to strengthen the mechanism.

2.1 Sliding Pivot: generating rocking motion

These are often used in conjunction with a Hub. In commercial pop-ups, the whole mechanism is usually hidden behind the page.

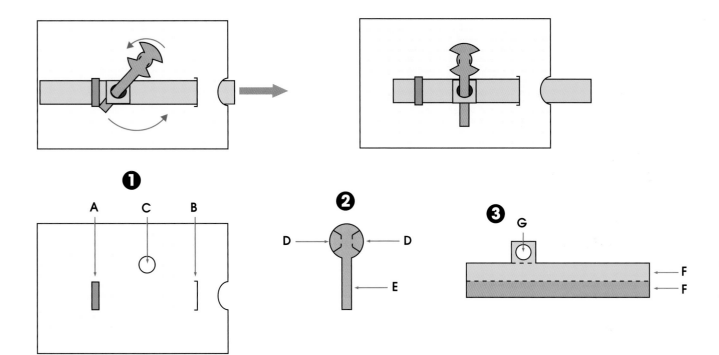

1 View of the back of the base card. It has a sleeve, **A**, and a slit, **B**, these both guide the Pull-strip and hold it to the page. The hole, **C**, is slightly more than $\frac{1}{2}$in (13mm) in diameter – the arms, **D**, of the Hub go through here. Put the Pull-strip as close to the hole as possible to generate maximum movement.

2 The Hub: This variation is constructed with a long arm, **E**, that is part of the Sliding Pivot. The arm should be at least double thickness, as the movement of the mechanism can put a lot of stress on it.

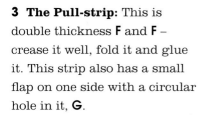

3 The Pull-strip: This is double thickness **F** and **F** – crease it well, fold it and glue it. This strip also has a small flap on one side with a circular hole in it, **G**.

4 Putting the pieces together: The arms on the Hub, **D** and **D**, go through the hole in the page, **C**, fold flat and have the image glued onto them. The flap, **G**, is folded over and arm **E** goes through it. The Pull-strip is threaded through the sleeve at one end and the slit at the other.

5 As the strip is pulled, the Hub rotates and arm **E** both turns and slides up and down through hole **G**.

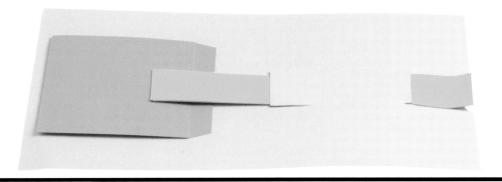

Pull-Tab Mechanism 3

Flaps

Pulling the tab makes the Flap flip over. This may simply be used to reveal an image; alternatively, a pop-up can be built into the gully formed between the Flap and the base. Pulling the tab can then be used to raise a three-dimensional construction anywhere on the page.

3.1 The Flap rises towards the Pull-strip

1 Make the Pull-strip double thickness and glue **A**.

2 The Flap is a plain piece of card with a gluing-tab on one side. Glue the Flap to the page, **B**.

3 Cut the two slits, **C** and **C**, in the page. The slits should be about ⅛in (3mm) wider than the Pull-strip. Note the shape of the slits – the ends should be curved back to allow the card to lift a little and so ease the movement of the Pull-strip.

4 Thread the Pull-strip through the slits. Glue the end of the strip to the Flap – **D**. Make sure that length **E** (between where the strip attaches to the Flap and where the Flap attaches to the page) is shorter than length **F** (between where the Flap attaches to the page and the nearest slit). If **F** is shorter than **E** the slit will inhibit the movement. **4 a** shows the position of the Flap and Pull-strip when the strip is in, and **4 b** the position of the Flap when the strip is pulled and the Flap has flipped over.

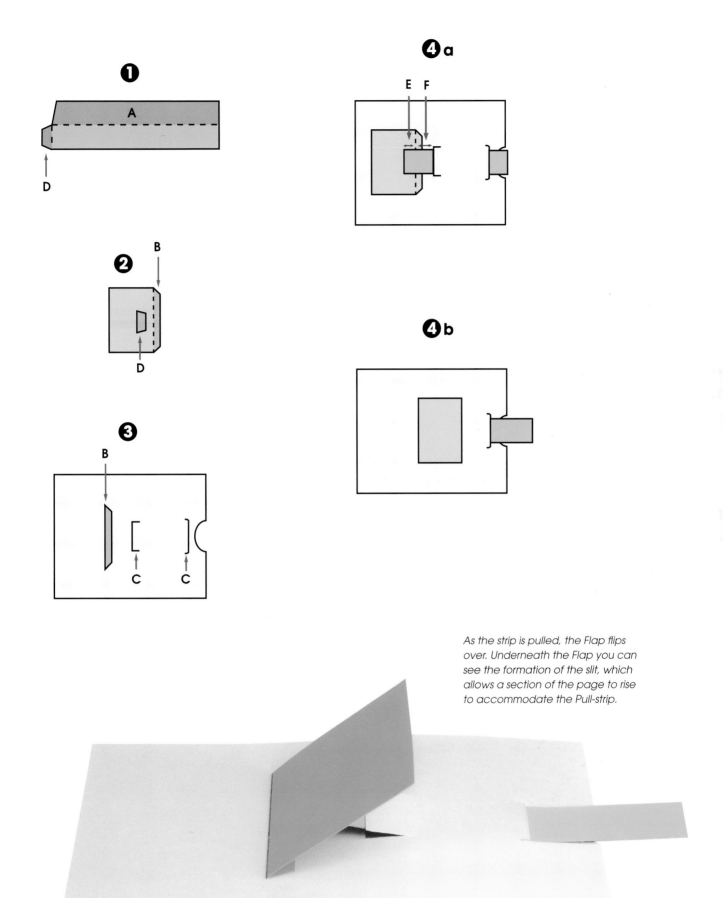

①

A

D

②

B

D

③

B

C C

④a

E F

④b

As the strip is pulled, the Flap flips over. Underneath the Flap you can see the formation of the slit, which allows a section of the page to rise to accommodate the Pull-strip.

3.2 The Flap rises away from the Pull-strip

This Flap is especially pleasing, as the entire mechanism is hidden away beneath the base. It is less robust than 3.1 and is slightly more difficult to make.

❶

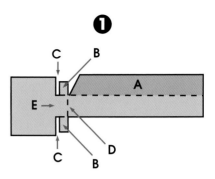

❷

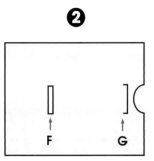

❹ ❺

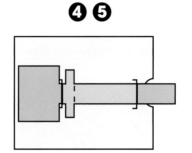

❻

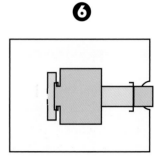

1 Make the Pull-strip and Flap out of one piece of card.

• Make the strip double thickness, fold over and glue **A**.

• There are two little Flaps **B**, between the Flap and the strip, separated from the Flap by two slots, **C**.

• The slots, **C**, are only ¹/₁₆in (2mm) wide, just enough to accommodate the thickness of the base-card.

• **D** is a fold, which goes across the Pull-strip, next to the Flaps **B**.

• **E** is the part of the piece that goes through the base-card. It is the weakest point on the whole piece. It may be reinforced with a small patch of card.

• The distance between **D** and **E** is normally ³/₈in (1cm).

• It is important not to confuse the position of **D** – it must not go between the slots **C** or the mechanism will not work.

2 Cut a slot in the base, **F**, ¹/₁₆in (2mm) wide and approximately ³/₁₆in (4mm) longer than the width of the Pull-strip. Cut slit **G**, also a little longer than the width of the strip.

3 Fold down the little Flaps **B** and thread the strip and the Flaps through the slot **F**.

4 Unfold the Flaps **B** and flatten them out at the back of the base. When the strip is pushed, these two now prevent the strip from sliding through the slot.

5 Thread the strip through the slit **G**.

6 Push the strip so that the Flap folds over and lies flat on the page. With the Flap in this position, trim off the end of the Pull-strip so that it is flush with the edge of the base.

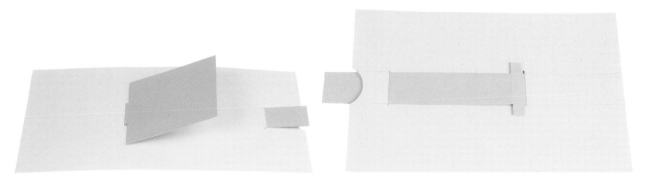

The top of the card with the Flap starting to lift.

The underside of the card showing two little tabs that stop the strip from sliding up through the slot when it's pushed.

3.3 Controlling the amount of movement

If the Flap is being used to raise a three-dimensional shape, it may be necessary to limit its movement. The amount that the flap moves can be governed by sticking an extra strip of card, **H**, across the Pull-strip. Then, when the strip is pulled, this additional piece will come up against the slit **G** and arrest the movement.

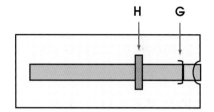

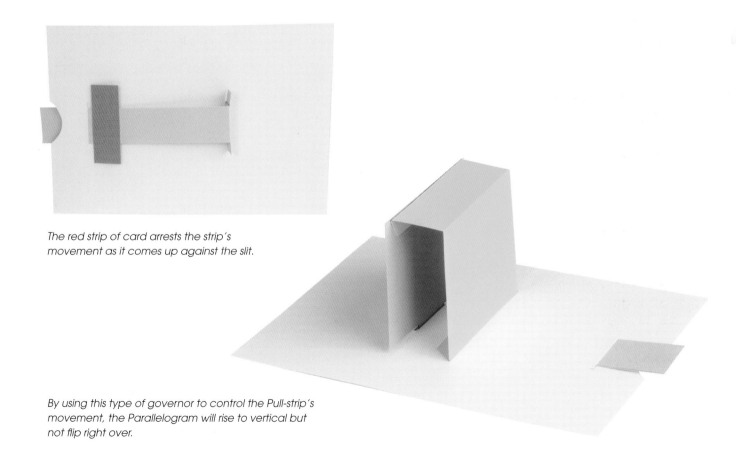

The red strip of card arrests the strip's movement as it comes up against the slit.

By using this type of governor to control the Pull-strip's movement, the Parallelogram will rise to vertical but not flip right over.

project templates

The following templates demonstrate how to build complex pop-ups.
General instructions for building these pop-ups are given on page 142.
The finished projects are illustrated on pages 142–145, together with
any instructions specifically relevant to each one. The actual templates
then follow. Your pop-ups may not look identical to those illustrated
but, providing the instructions are followed carefully, they will work.
The projects can be modified by adjusting lengths and angles, or by gluing
pieces on at different angles. They can be decorated in your own way;
painting or drawing is best done before the pieces are cut out, while
glued-on decorations (such as card, tissue paper, photos, fabric, feathers,
foil and leaves) should be added after the model is finished.

General guidelines

To make these models you will need card, scissors, craft-knife, glue, ruler, pencil and a scoring implement – if you wish to modify a design, you will also need a set square, protractor and compass (see further details in 'Materials' on pages 14–15).

1 Copy the designs on to card. You can do this either by photocopying (most easy), tracing (this will need some care), or measuring all the lengths and angles and drawing up the design yourself.

2 Score all the folds, then cut out the pieces.

3 Thoroughly fold and crimp the fold lines. All dotted lines are Valley-folds. All dashed lines are Mountain-folds. (See 'Terms used', on page 13.)

4 Before starting to glue, check that the base is very well creased; read the text beside the relevant photograph on the following pages and, if necessary, look up the relevant Foundation Shape and Building Technique.

5 Before gluing a tab, hold the piece in place and check that it will fit – for example, if a tab is slightly too big, so that it crosses over the spine, trim a little piece off.

6 Gluing: follow the order marked on the tabs and smear glue right up to the crease. After adding each piece, close the base and press firmly to ensure that it is sound. If there is a problem, pull the piece off quickly before the glue has fully set, make adjustments, then glue it down again.

7 Where a piece is glued together before it is attached to the base or model, ensure that it can fold flat before attaching it.

Project 1 HOUSE
(templates on pp. 146–147)

Based on a **Right-angle V-fold** raising **Parallelograms**. As the spread closes, the walls twist in relation to the roof. A 'roof beam' in a vertical position between the two gable ends creates another **Parallelogram** which the roof itself can be attached to.

Project 2 GARDEN
(templates on pp. 148–149)

Based on a **Right-angle V-fold**, which raises a **Parallelogram** built into its vertical gully. A second **Parallelogram** is built into the gully created where the first one joins the **V-fold**. Glue the 'hedges' into place, then add the other 'plants' to suit your individual design.

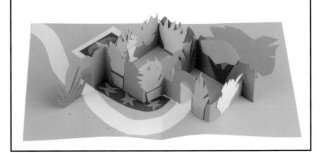

Project 3 LUNCH
(templates on pp. 150–151)

An **Acute-angle V-fold** has two **Counter-folds** cut into the tabs that attach it to the page – these **Counter-folds** raise the arms. A small **Pointed V-fold** forms the nose. The gluing-tabs attaching the pop-up piece to the page have been modified: one half goes back, behind the pop-up, the other half comes forward.

Project 4 HORSE
(templates on pp. 152–153)

A **Parallel-fold** forms the main body of the horse. The neck has a wedge cut out to fit over the horse's body, the other end has tabs for attaching the head. An **Angle-folded strip** forms the tail, which glues into the underside of the body. The angles at which the neck, head and tail are attached can all be varied.

Project 5 DANCERS
(templates on pp. 154–155)

Two **Parallelograms** (the first built into the gully of the spine, the second built into a gully created by the first one) move multiple arms. The arms and legs on the template provide the basic shapes that can be 'dressed'. As each new piece is added, close the base to make sure that the new piece isn't snagging.

Project 6 AEROPLANE
(templates on pp. 156–157)

An **M-fold** forms the clouds with two tabs on the top of one of the gullies supporting the plane (based on a **Curved shape**). Glue the 'clouds' to the page first. Before gluing the plane to the cloud, experiment with its angle in the gully: make sure the central fold of the plane sits snugly in the gully and close the base while the glue is still soft to make sure that the wings are sufficiently flat. (See 'Using angled creases to make gluing-tabs', on page 105.)

Project 7 RECLINING FIGURE
(templates on pp. 158–159)

An **Acute-angle V-fold** forms the main body with a **Counter-fold** making the top arm. The head is another **Acute V-fold**, while the lower arm is a **Parallelogram**.

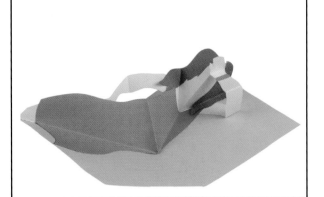

Project 8 BIRD
(templates on pp. 160–161)

A **Floating plane**. The head is a simple **Curved shape** glued into the gully above the page. The tail is an **Angle-folded strip** glued into the gully underneath the centre of the **Floating plane**. The angle of the creases on the tail can be changed to create a different shape.

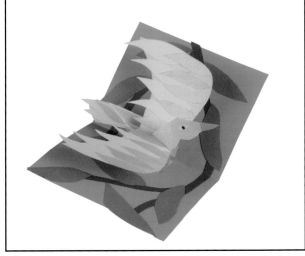

Project 9 BOAT
(templates on pp. 162–163)

This is a **Box** with the ends modified to create the boat shape. Glue the mast in between the two layers of card that form the central 'pillar' of the box.

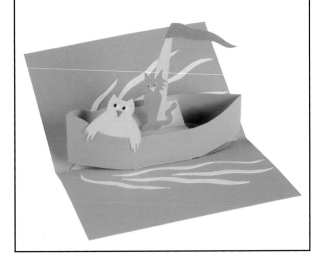

Project 10 FLOWER
(templates on pp. 164–165)

Open-topped shapes with a hexagonal **Pyramid** in the middle. Glue the outer (white) ring into place first, then the pink and finally the yellow. The gluing-tabs all stick down in the same two places on top of each other.

Project 11 FISH
(templates on pp. 166–167)

A **Curved shape** forms the main body of the fish and two **Slots** accommodate the fins, which are glued to the inside of the body. The tail is an **Angle-folded strip** – change the angle of the creases to modify the shape.

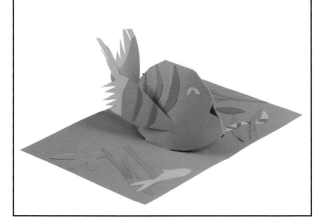

Project 12 RUNNER
(templates on pp. 168–169)

This is a **Twisting mechanism** with its various planes extended to form the limbs.

Project 13 CAR
(templates on pp. 170–171)

Based on the **Moving-arm** mechanisms, opening the page turns the wheels. The underlying **Parallelogram** has been modified to generate two 'corners' for building on. Small 'L'-shaped pieces fit on to the triangles that would support **Moving arms**. The wheels are glued to the other ends of the 'L'-shapes. The body of the vehicle forms another **Parallelogram** – one end glued to the page, the other attached to the top face of the underlying structure.

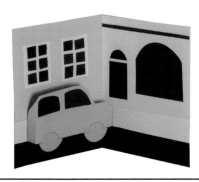

Project 14 DRAGON
(templates on pp. 172–173)

A double **45-degree fold** forms the basic structure. Two **Angle-folded strips** form the head and tail: the angles of the folds on these can be altered to modify the shape.

Project 1 HOUSE (see model on page 142)

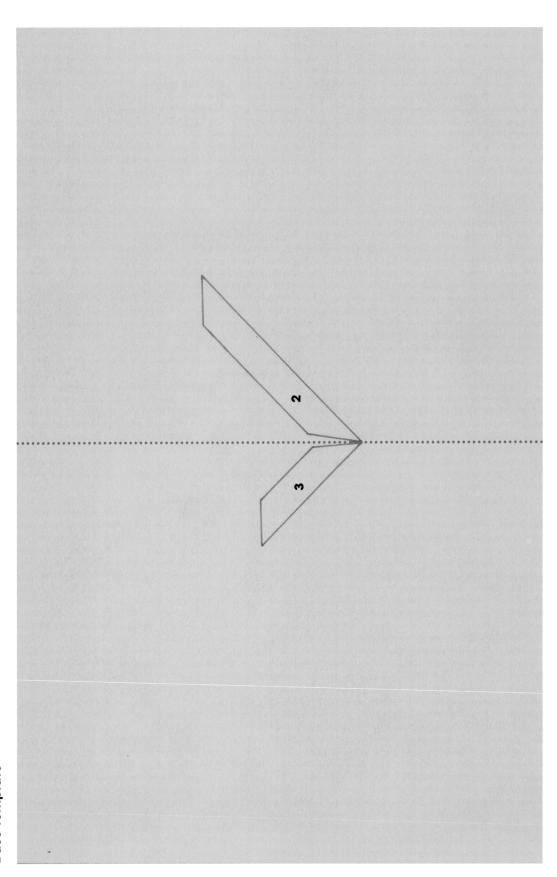

House template

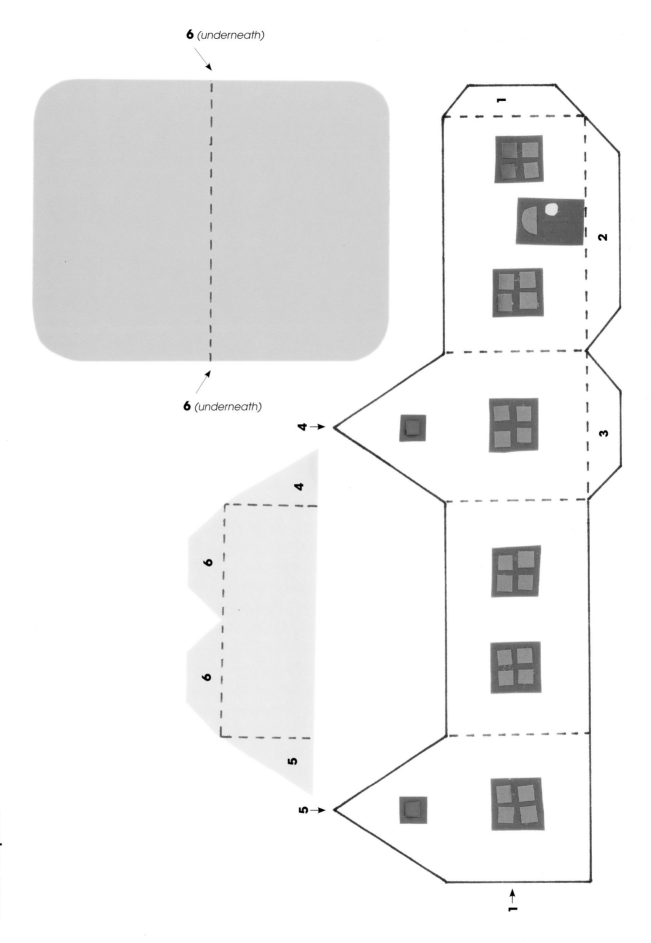

6 *(underneath)*

6 *(underneath)*

1

2

3

4

4

6

6

5

5

1

Project 2 GARDEN (see model on page 142)

Garden template

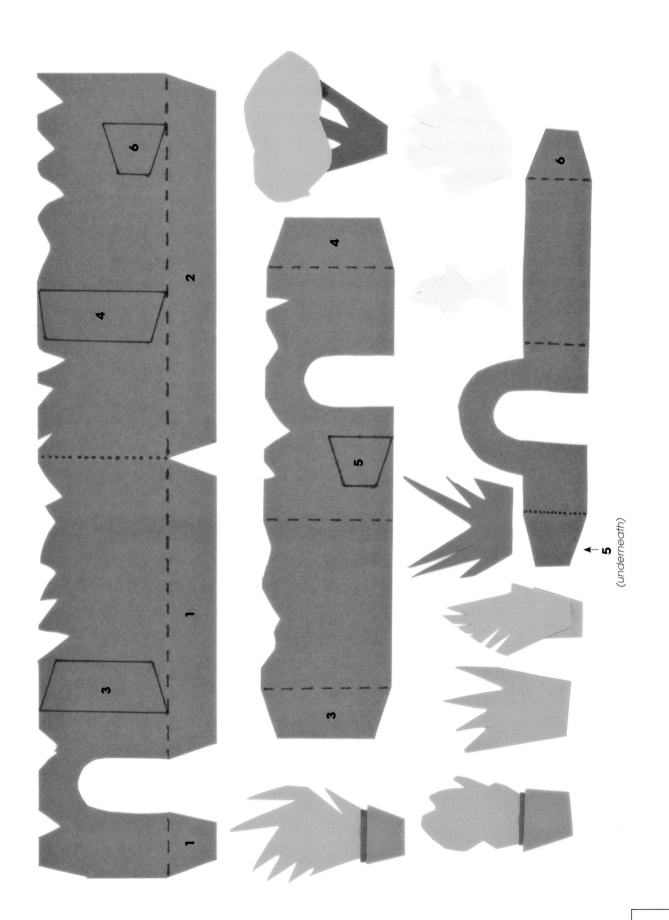

(underneath)

Project 3 LUNCH (see model on page 143)

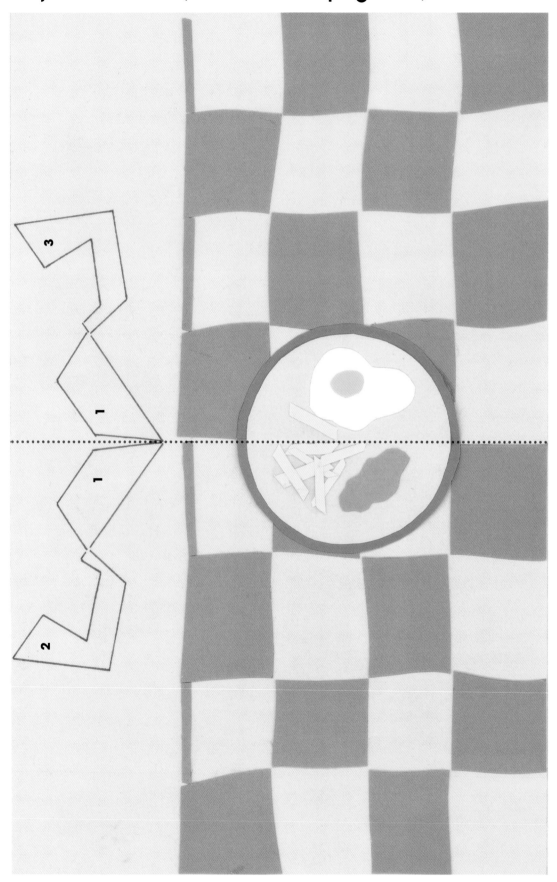

Lunch template

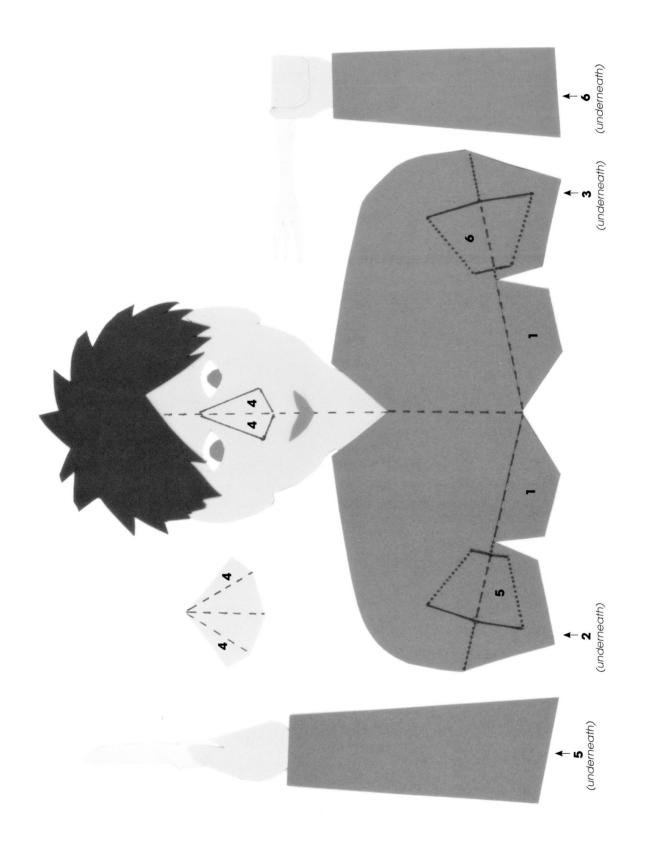

Project 4 HORSE (see model on page 143)

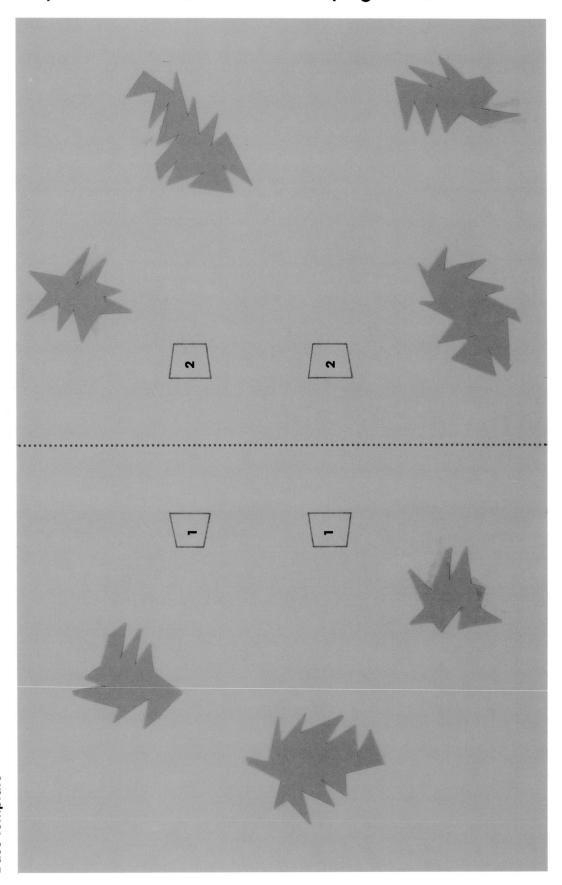

Pop-up Design and Paper Mechanics

Horse template

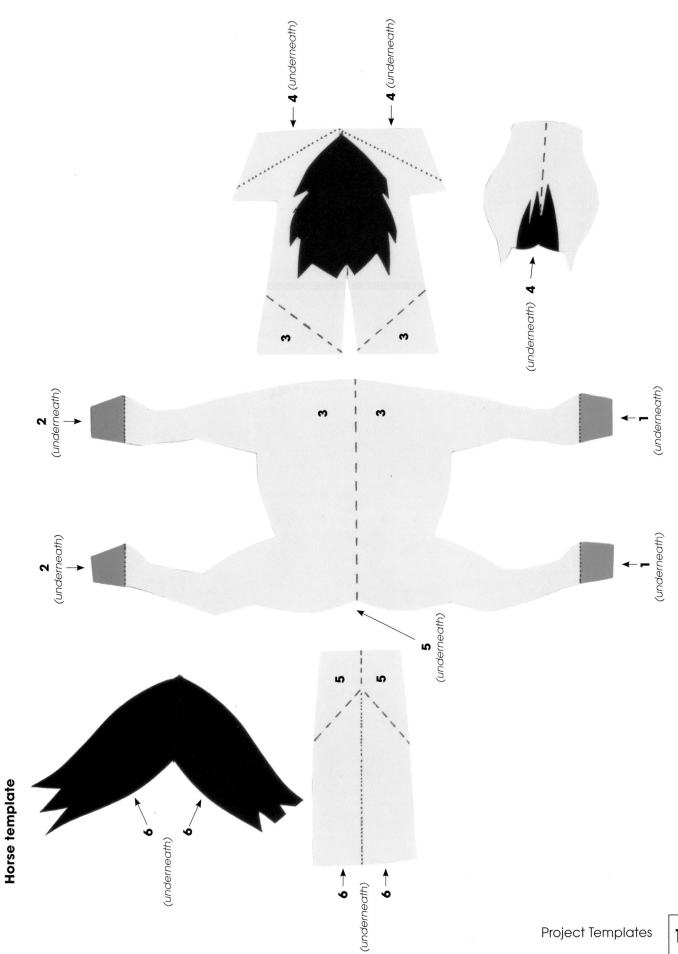

Project 5 DANCERS (see model on page 143)

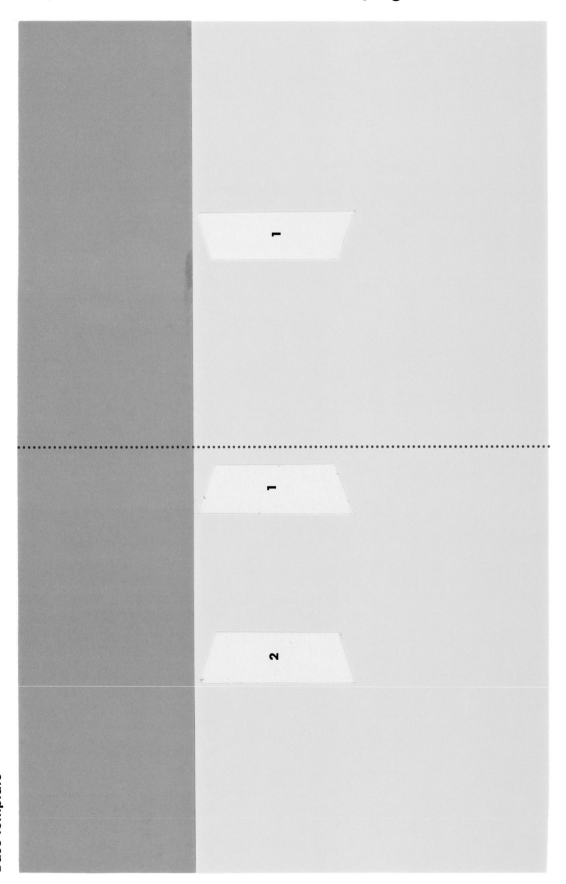

Pop-up Design and Paper Mechanics

Base template

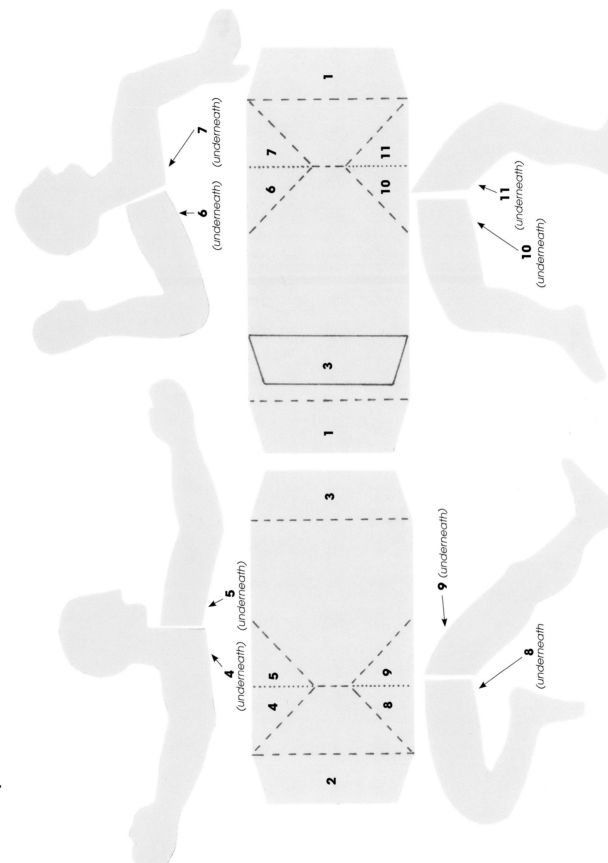

The limbs provide a structure that can be dressed in individual style.

Project 6 AEROPLANE (see model on page 143)

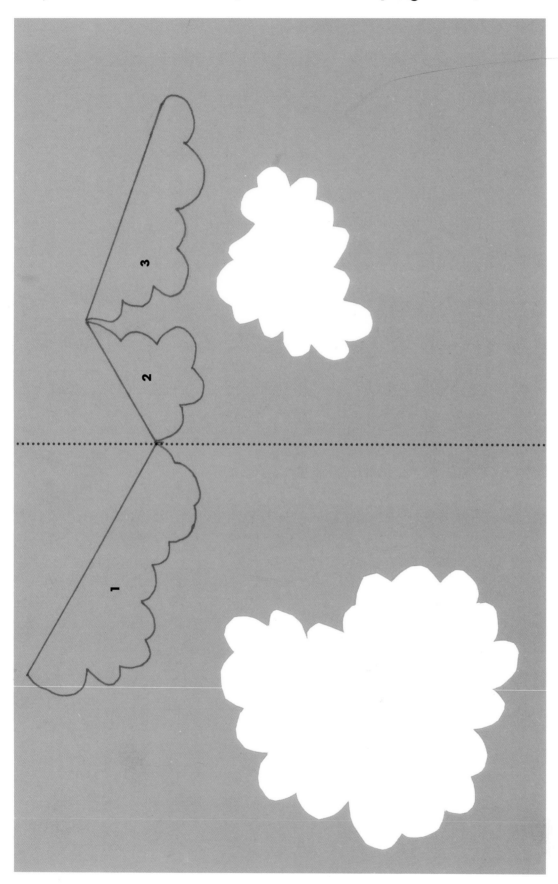

Aeroplane template

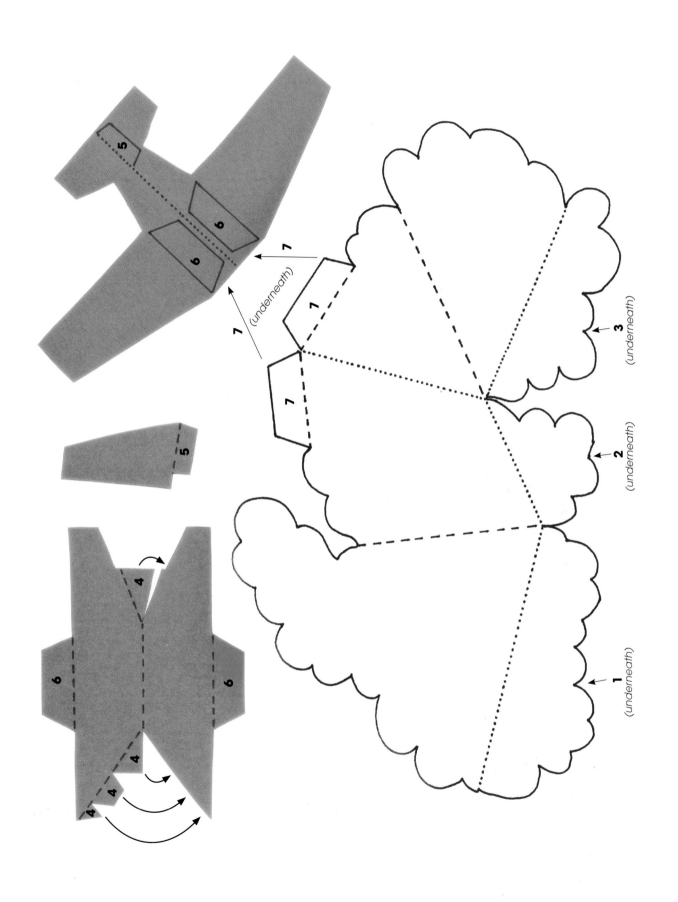

5

6

6

7

7 (underneath)

7

7

7

5

4

4

4

4

6

6

3 (underneath)

2 (underneath)

1 (underneath)

Project 7 RECLINING FIGURE (see model on page 144)

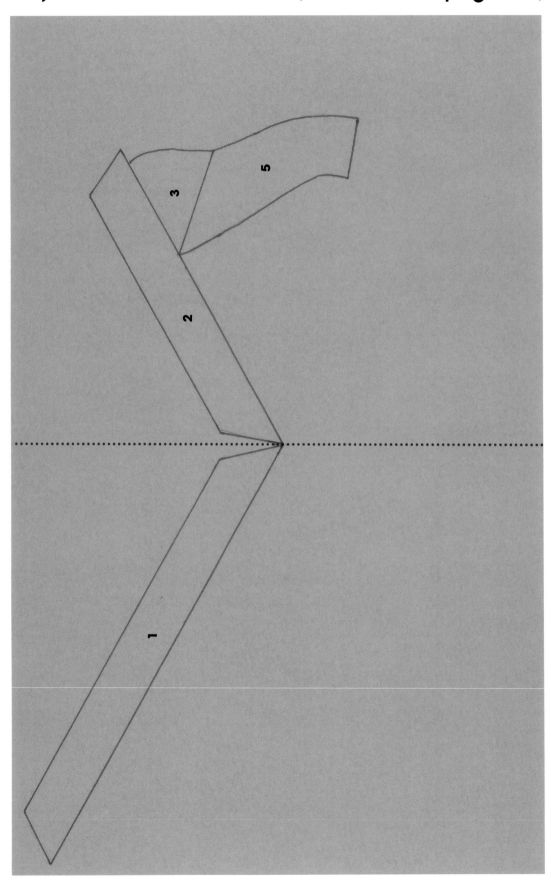

Base template

Figure template

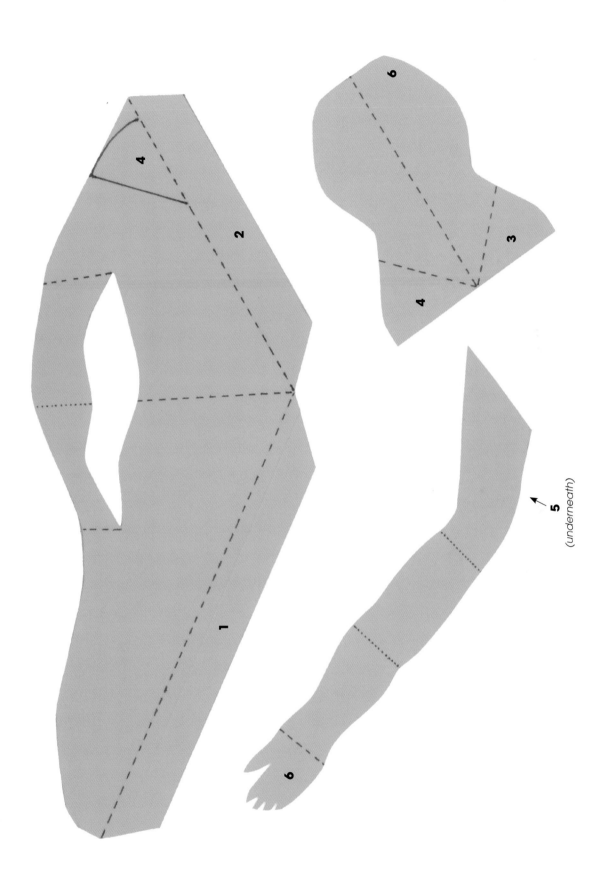

Project 8 BIRD (see model on page 144)

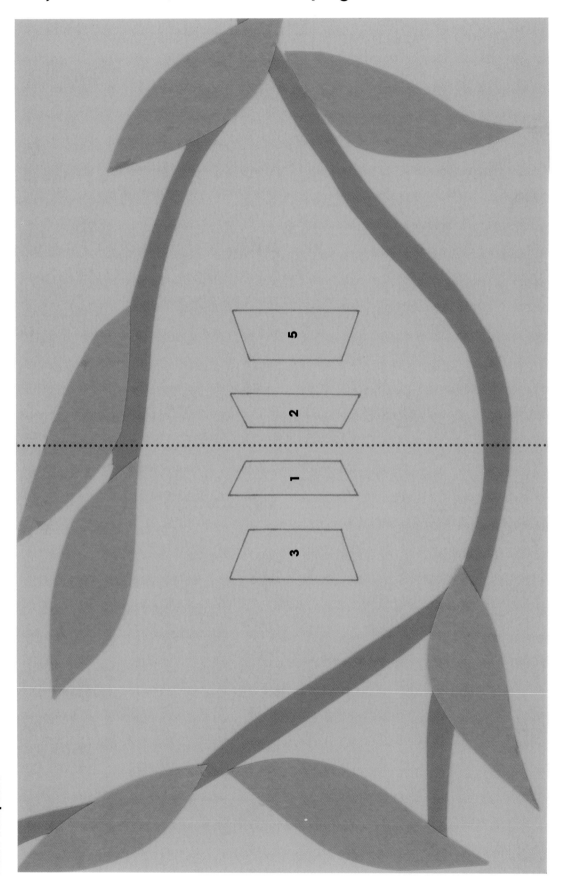

Bird template

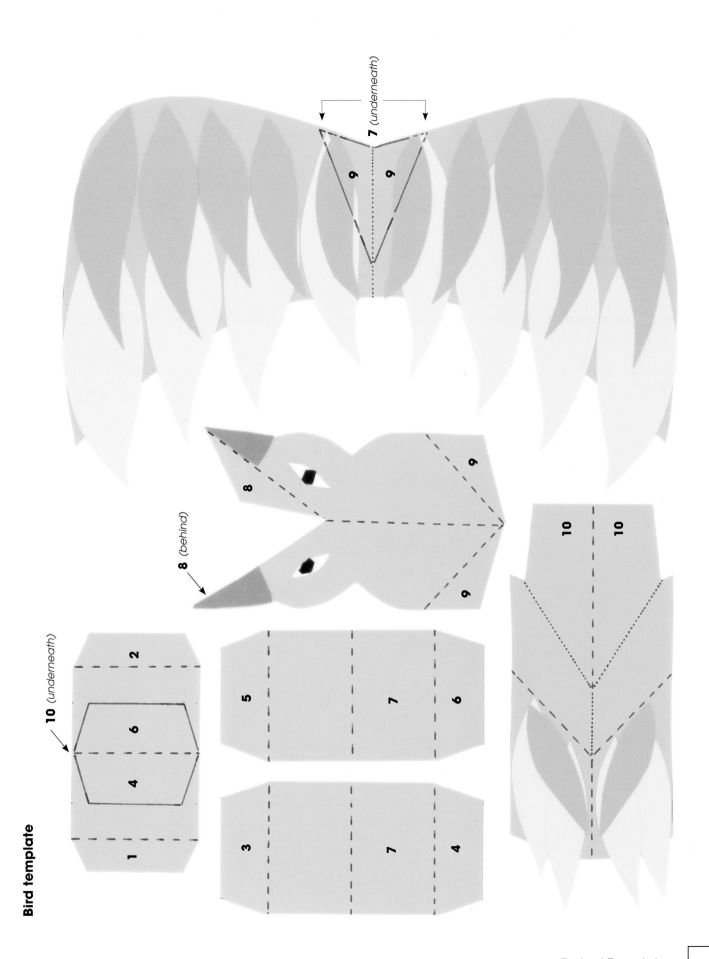

Project 9 BOAT (see model on page 144)

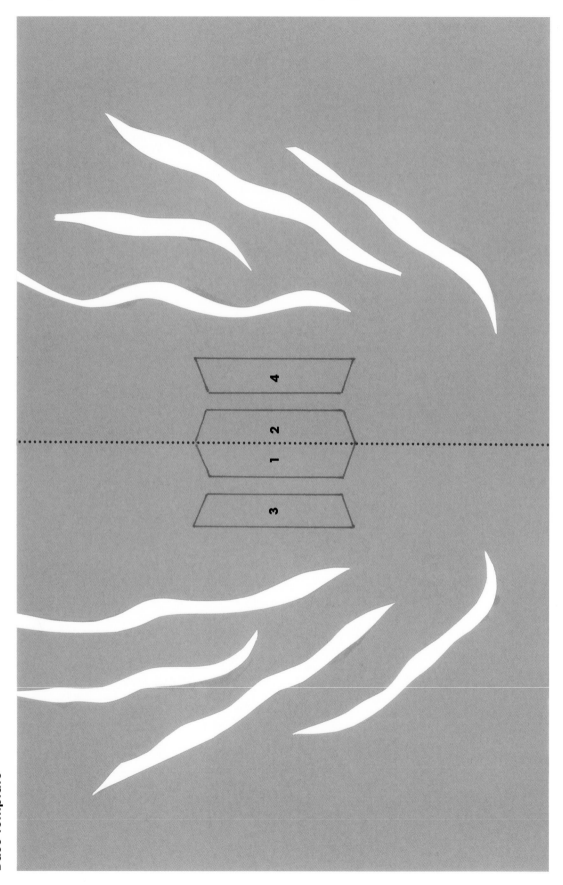

Boat template

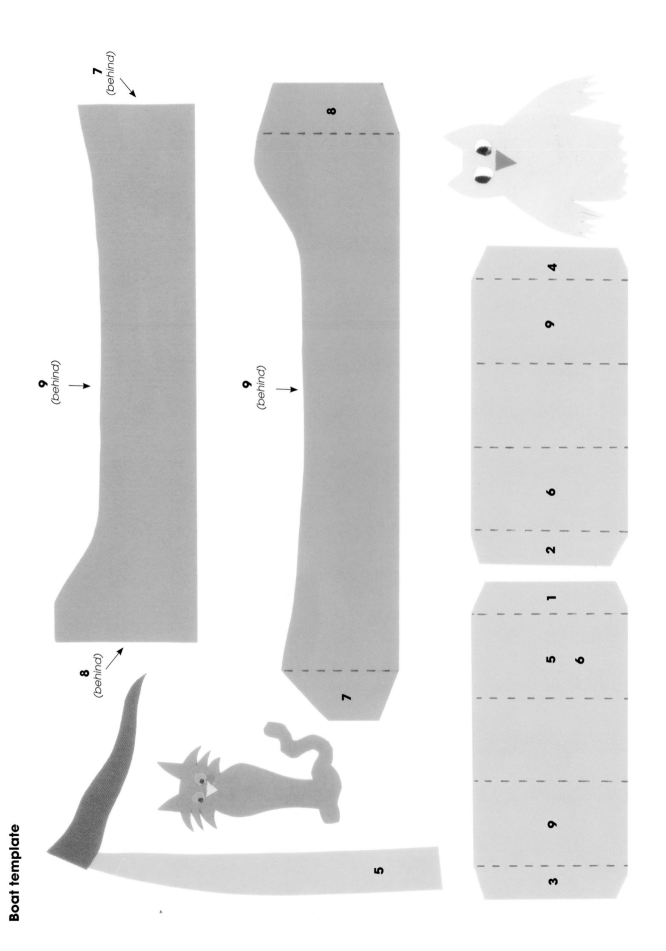

Project 10 FLOWER (see model on page 144)

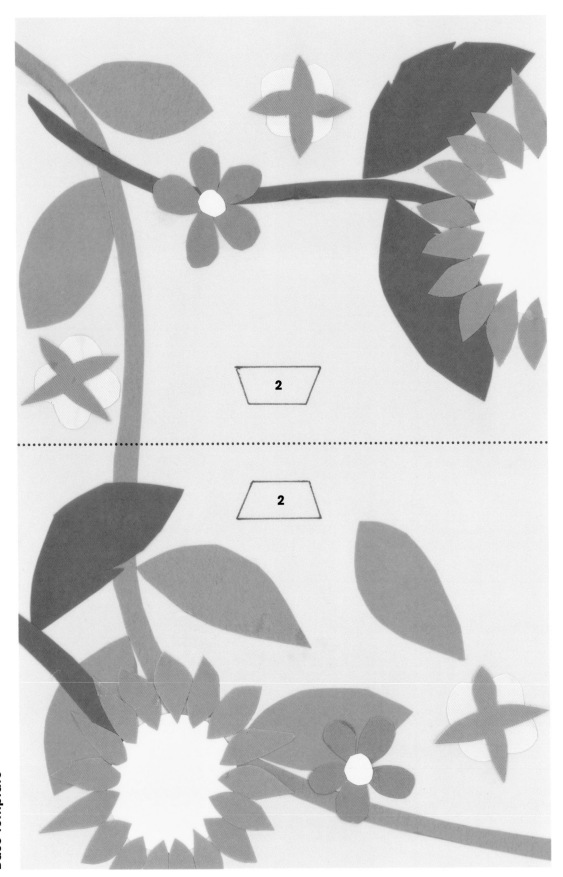

Pop-up Design and Paper Mechanics

Flower template

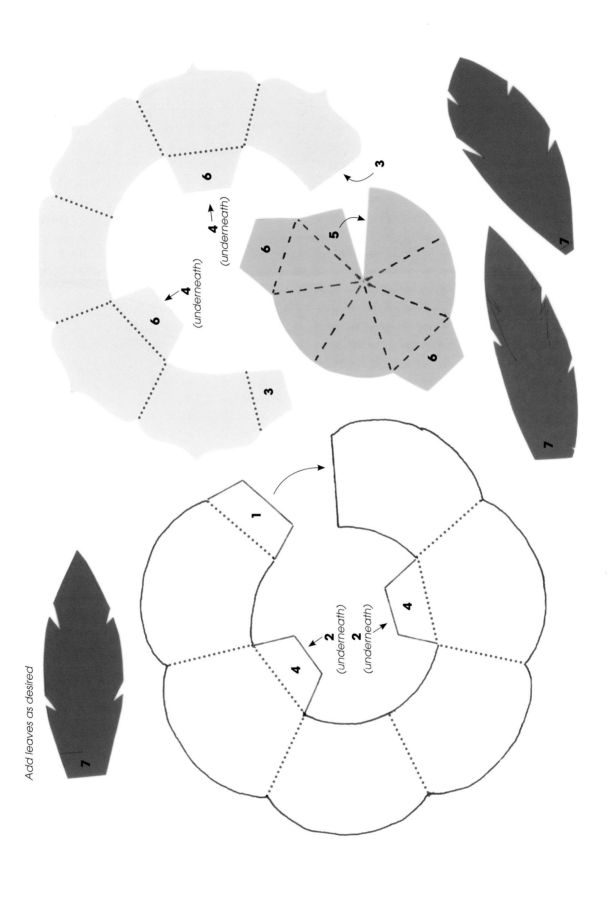

Add leaves as desired

Project 11 FISH (see model on page 145)

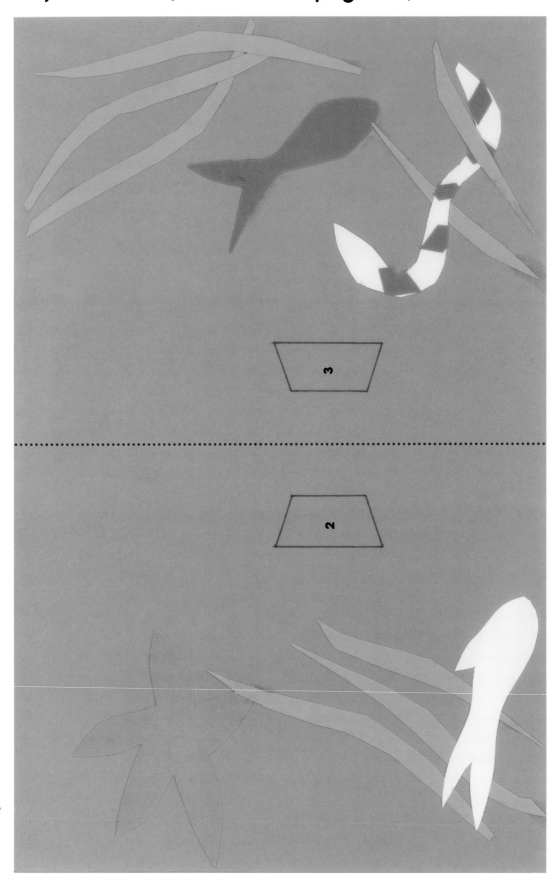

Pop-up Design and Paper Mechanics

Fish template

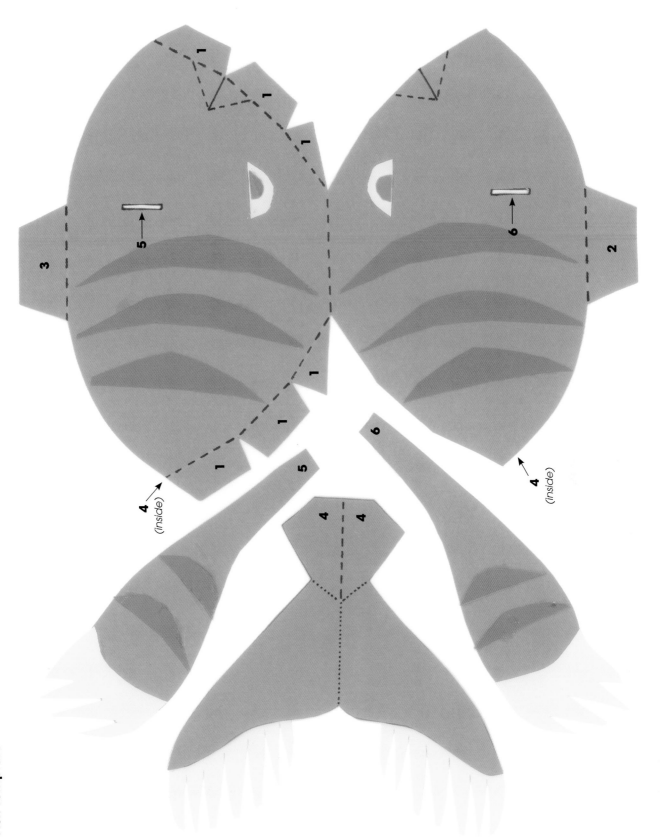

Project 12 RUNNER (see model on page 145)

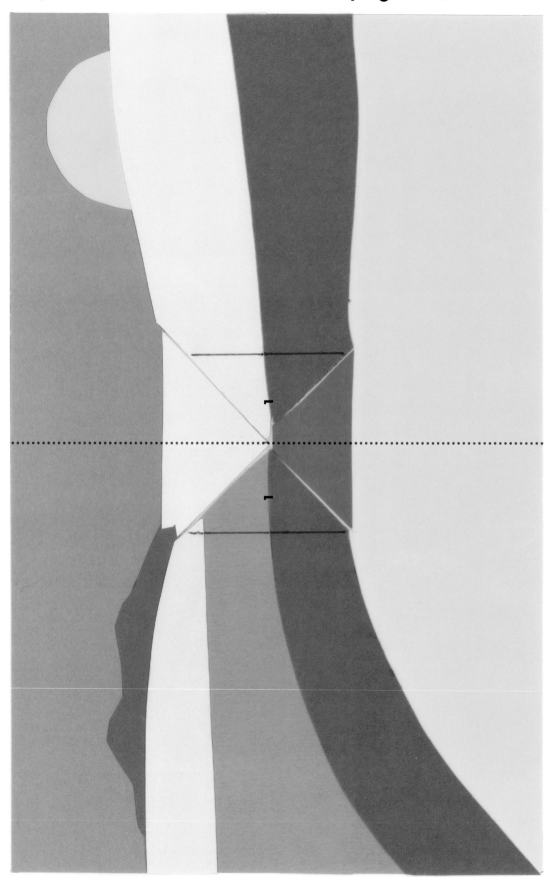

Runner template

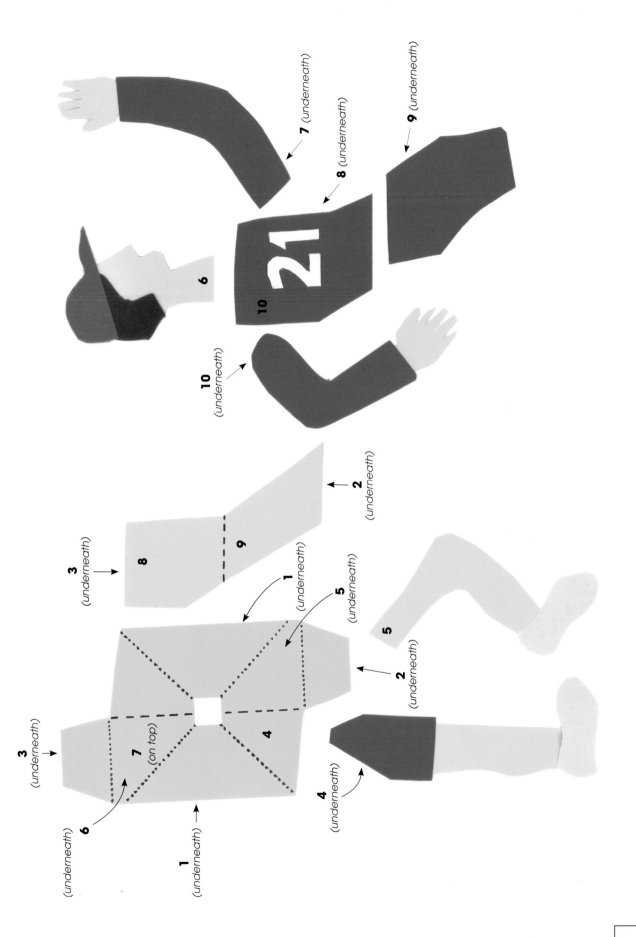

Project 13 CAR (see model on page 145)

Car template

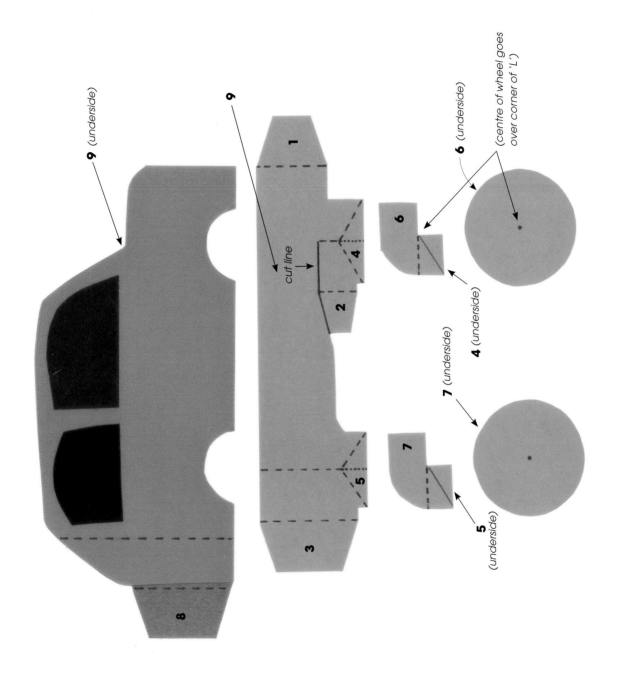

9 (underside)

9

cut line

1

4

2

3

5

6

6 (underside)

(centre of wheel goes over corner of 'L')

4 (underside)

7 (underside)

7

5

5 (underside)

8

Project 14 DRAGON (see model on page 145)

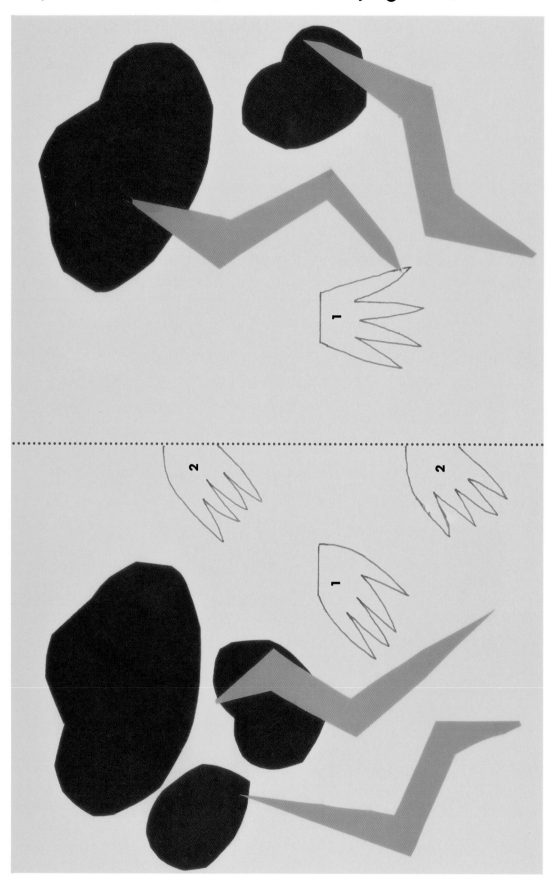

Pop-up Design and Paper Mechanics

Dragon template

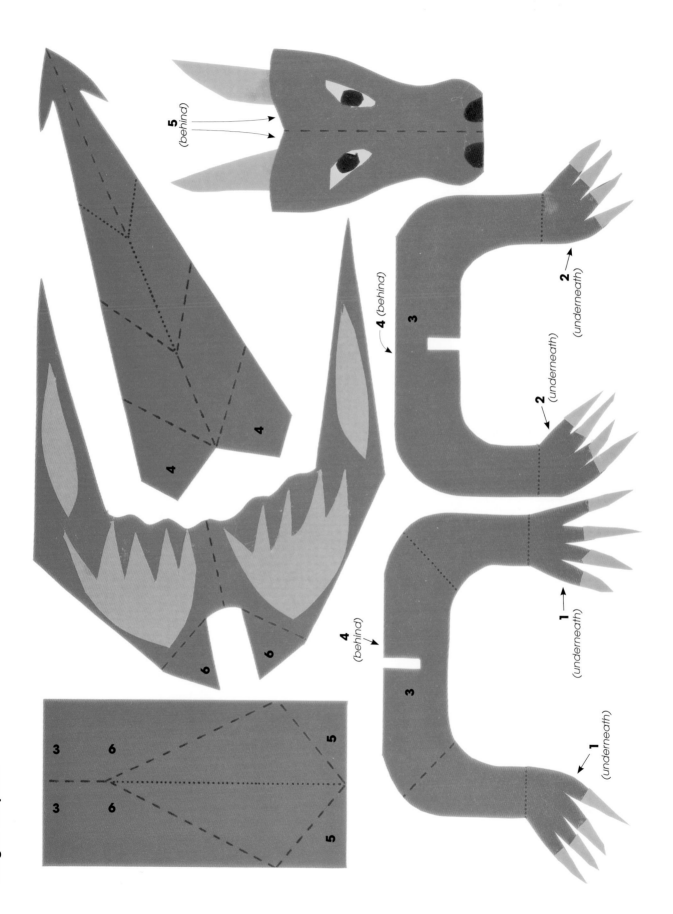

About the author

Duncan Birmingham has been teaching the intriguing art of pop-up since 1989. He currently teaches Illustration degree students at the University of the West of England, gives one-day workshops for secondary school teachers countrywide and has also taught junior school, GCSE and adult education classes in this country and abroad. He enjoys enabling others to create and experiment with this unusual skill, and is continually inspired by the work and enthusiasm of his students.

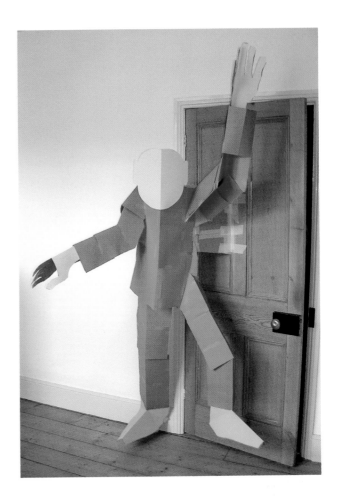

His previous pop-up publications include *The Maya, Aztecs and Incas Pop-Up*, which follows his interest in ancient civilizations, and *Cut-and-Make Pop-Up Cards*. His exhaustive *Pop-Up! A Manual of Paper Mechanisms* has been praised by one of the world's top paper engineers, as 'The most thorough book to date on the subject. Excellent for those serious about commercial, complex pop-ups.'

Duncan studied Art at the School of Expressive Arts, Sonoma State University in California and at Central Saint Martins College of Art and Design in London, England (*formerly* Saint Martins School of Art and Design). He has also worked as an illustrator, designed geometry posters for schools and is the creator of the popular children's puzzle book '*M' is for Mirror*. Before discovering the world of pop-ups his other experiences included a variety of jobs: on archaeological digs, backstage at West End theatres, on a dairy farm, bee keeping, and boat building.

Aside from pop-up, Duncan's other great interest is travel. Over more than 30 years he has made numerous sustained overland journeys to iconic and legendary places in Africa, the Americas, the Middle East and Asia.

He is married and lives in Bristol, south-west England. More of Duncan's work can be seen on his website: **www.duncanbirmingham.co.uk**

Index

A

Acute-angle V-fold **20**
    method **32-3**
acute angles (term) **13**
adhesive
    types **14**
    working practice **17**
Aeroplane **143, 156-7**
Angle-folded strips **106-7**
Angled creases, adding extra **102-5**
Arch, cutting from V-fold **96**
Asymmetric Parallel-fold **21**
    method **50-1**
Asymmetric V-fold **20**
    method **38-41**
Automatic pull-strips **23**
    basic method **82-3**
building on to Parallelogram **86**
    to raise flap in middle of page **85**
    running under the page **84**
    theory **86**
    turning flap on opposite page **87**

B

base-cards **13**
    making **17**
Bending planes **122-3**
Bird **144, 160-1**
Boat **144, 162-3**
Box **22**
    basic method **64-6**
    box top **129**
    Cylindrical Box **67**
building techniques
    45-degree folds **126-9**
    Angle-folded strips **106-7**
    Bending planes **122-3**
    checklist **95**
    Counter-folds **108-15**
    cutting parts away **96-7**
    extra creases **102-5**
    Slots **116-21**
    sticking pieces on **98-101**
    Straps **124-5**

C

Car **145, 170-1**
card **14, 16**
cartridge paper **14, 16**
compasses **15**
Cone **75**
Counter-folds **108-15**
craft-knives **15**
Curved shapes **23**
    basic method **76-9**
cutting, working practice **16**
cutting-mats **15**
cutting parts away **96-7**

D

Dancers **143, 154-5**
Dragon **145, 172-3**
drawing instruments **15**
dummy **13**

E

erasers **15**

F

45-degree folds **126-9**
Fish **145, 166-7**
Flaps **136-9**
Floating plane **22**
    method **60-3**
Flower **144, 164-5**
folding, working practice **16**

G

Garden **142, 148-9**
glue
    types **14**
    working practice **17**
gluing-tabs **13**
    angled creases as **105**
    working practice **16**
gullies **13**
    rules for **18-19**

H

Horse **143, 152-3**
House **142, 146-7**
Hub **134**

L

Lunch **143, 150-1**

M

M-fold **22**
    method **56-9**
materials **14-15**
measuring
    awkward angles **27**
    working practice **16**
mechanism (term) **13**
Mountain-fold **13, 56, 97, 106, 142**
Moving arms **23**
    attached to base **93**
    glued to outer gully **90-1**
    powered by Parallelogram **88-9**
    powered by V-fold and Counter-fold **92**

N

nets **13**
    drawing up **26**

O

Obtuse-angle V-fold **20**
    method **36-7**
obtuse angles **13**
Open-topped shapes **23**
    add a lid **129**
    basic method **68-9**
    rectangular variation **71**
    square **69**
    tapered variations **70**
    on a V-fold **71**

P

Parallel-fold 21
  adding Parallel-fold pieces 98-9
  basic method 42-4
  curved variations 45
  simple rules of 18-19
  see also Asymmetric Parallel-fold;
        Parallelogram
Parallelogram 13, 21
  basic method 46-7
  building on to V-folds 48-9
  'filling in' the end of 128
pencils 15
photocopy card 16
Pivots 134-5
plane (term) 13
Pointed V-fold 20
  method 34-5
pop-up sketching 24-5
  converting to pop-ups 26-7
projects
  Aeroplane 143, 156-7
  Bird 144, 160-1
  Boat 144, 162-3
  Car 145, 170-1
  Dancers 143, 154-5
  Dragon 145, 172-3
  Fish 145, 166-7
  Flower 144, 164-5
  Garden 142, 148-9
  Horse 143, 152-3
  House 142, 146-7
  Lunch 143, 150-1
  Reclining Figure 144, 158-9
  Runner 145, 168-9
protractors 15
pull-tab mechanisms 131
  Flaps 136-9
  Pivots 134-5
  Pull-strips 132-3

Pyramid 23
  basic method 72-3
  Asymmetric Pyramid 74
  Cone 75
  Elongated Pyramid 73
  Parallel-fold Pyramid 73

Q

quadrilateral (term) 13

R

Reclining Figure 144, 158-9
Right-angle V-fold 20
  method 30-1
right angles (term) 13
rulers 15
Runner 145, 168-9

S

scissors 14
score lines (term) 13
scoring 15, 16
set squares 15
sketches 24-5
  converting to pop-ups 26-7
Sliding Pivot 135
Slits 13
Slots 13, 116-21
spine-fold (term) 13
Spirals 122-3
spread (term) 13
sticking pieces on 98-101
sticking strip 13
Straps 124-5

T

terms 13
Twisting mechanism 23
  method 80-1

V

V-fold 13
  adding V-fold pieces 100-1
  simple rules of 18-19
  see also Acute-angle V-fold; Asymmetric
        V-fold; Obtuse-angle V-fold;
        Pointed V-fold; Right-angle
        V-fold
Valley-fold 13, 56, 106, 142

W

working order 27

Z

Zigzag-fold 22
  basic method 52-3
  with angled secondary folds 54
  asymmetric variation 55

To request a full catalogue of GMC titles, please contact:

GMC Publications Ltd

Castle Place, 166 High Street, Lewes, East Sussex, BN7 1XU, United Kingdom
Tel: +44 (0)1273 488005   Fax: +44 (0)1273 402866   www.thegmcgroup.com

Orders by credit card are accepted